CULTURAL ENCOUNTERS IN THE USA
CROSS-CULTURAL DIALOGUES AND MINI-DRAMAS

Many thanks to Teri Flynn and David Tillyer for their encouragement and insight.

Contents

Introduction			v
How to Use This Book			vii
1.	Sunday Football	Sports, Television	1
2.	One of the Family	Meals, Guest behavior	2
3.	Everyday Meals	Meals, Daily life	3
4.	Wine with Dinner	Meals, Laws	4
5.	Independence Day	Special days	5
6.	What's On?	Television	6
7.	The Right Way to Drive	Driving, Laws	7
8.	Starting High School	School	8
9.	Sandwiches to Go	Meals, Stores	9
10.	At the Checkout Counter	Stores	10
11.	Participating in Class	School, Social interaction	11
12.	An Innocent Hug	Social interaction	12
13.	Private Thoughts	Social interaction, Sports	13
14.	Here Comes the Bride	Weddings, Traditions	14
15.	Strong Coffee	Stores	15
16.	Dinner at Eight	Meals, Guest behavior, Formality	16
17.	Just Call Me Erica	Greetings, Names, Formality	17
18.	Bargain Hunting	Shopping, Stores	18
19.	How Much Should I Leave?	Tipping, Meals	19
20.	Proud of Their Heritage	Ethnicity	20
21.	A Riddle	Stereotypes, Family	21
22.	Traveling by Train	Traveling, Idiomatic language	22
23.	How Cold Is It?	Weather, Seasons	23
24.	A Birthday on a Beach	Special days, Weather	24
25.	What to Wear	Clothing, Formality	25
26.	A Traditional Christmas	Special days, Traditions	26
27.	Walking the Dog	Animals, Meals	27
28.	All You Can Eat	Meals	28
29.	I Need This Vacation	Social Interaction, Vacations	29
30.	Nicknames	Names, Formality	30
31.	A Death in the Family	Death, Family	31
32.	Really?	Compliments, Social interaction	32

33.	Is It a Date?	Social interaction	33
34.	The Right Size	Stores, Sizes	34
35.	Sorry I'm Late	Social interaction, Punctuality	35
36.	At the Mall	Social awareness, Stores	36
37.	Trick or Treat	Special days, Traditions	37
38.	Getting a Ticket	Laws	38
39.	The Missing Floor	Superstition, Traditions	39
40.	Many Colors	Ethnicity	40
41.	Going Dutch	Social interaction, Money	41
42.	How Much Do You Make?	Social interaction, Money	42
43.	Table Manners	Meals, Guest behavior	43
44.	Summer Sun	Vacations	44
45.	Dressed for the Occasion	Clothing, Formality, Social interaction	45
46.	No Smoking	Smoking, Meals	46
47.	Designated Driver	Drinking, Driving	47
48.	The Right to Work	Jobs	48
49.	On the Highway	Driving, Directions	49
50.	A Bit Crowded	Social interaction	50
51.	Stage Fright	Idiomatic language	51
52.	Seven Years of Bad Luck	Traditions, Superstition	52

Follow-ups	55
Topical Index	109
Vocabulary	115

Introduction

Cultural Encounters in the U.S.A. is designed to expand cultural awareness while assisting in the study of English. In a world brought ever closer by jet travel and modern telecommunications, this book fills a distinct and important need. Increasingly, men and women come into contact with different cultures and have to learn the occasionally difficult lesson of how to communicate with one another. These encounters with people from different countries or cultures can be full of surprises and cause unforeseen problems.

Each of the fifty-two mini-dramas in this book deals directly with such cultural dilemmas and illustrates the fact that values, attitudes, lifestyles, expectations, beliefs, and roles tend to be perceived in different ways in different countries. At the end of each mini-drama, students are asked a question regarding the cultural conflict presented and are given four possible solutions. They check their answers. If they choose an incorrect answer the first time, they are given clues and further information to help them find the correct solutions. (See the section "How to Use This Book" for a more detailed description.) The explanations give important and interesting information on understanding aspects of North American culture, including daily life, business, family, school, and social situations.

These mini-dramas can be used as supplementary material, as a self-study text, or as a mini-course. Since they are self-contained, the various concepts treated may be discussed in the order in which they arise in the basal text in the class. For classroom use, the fifty-two mini-dramas in *Cultural Encounters in the U.S.A.* may be used at a rate of about one a week during a single school year, or two a week over a semester.

Each mini-drama explores an aspect of one or two main topics. For each mini-drama, topics are specified in the table of contents and also in the topical index provided for convenient reference at the back of the book. The topical index is not exhaustive and lessons are included under the broadest topics relating to them. While the mini-dramas focus on specific topics, they also offer opportunity to discuss related topics. For example, the mini-drama "No Smoking," which involves the topic of smoking, presents an ideal opportunity to discuss the related issues of health and individual versus group rights. You may want to add to the list of topics for future use.

Three basic objectives guided the preparation of this cultural material:

1. Students will recognize and appreciate that cultural differences—not just language differences—exist between and within cultures;

2. students traveling to Canada or the United States will experience fewer difficulties due to cultural conflict; and

3. if a cultural conflict does occur, the student will be able to resolve it intelligently because of previous experience testing hypotheses. With this preparation, the consequences of cultural shock will be minimized.

In connection with these cultural mini-dramas, teachers may lead students in a discussion that brings out the relative nature of cultural expressions. Such a discussion could make the point that there is no one "right" way of thinking or acting—that there may be a variety of legitimate responses. For additional work, students might continue a dialogue at the point where the foreigner in the story begins to understand. Students might also write new mini-dramas that show the foreigner responding appropriately to the situation.

Cultural Encounters in the U.S.A.
* encourages students to deepen their knowledge of English and North American culture.
* promotes increased understanding of cultural diversity.

Other National Textbook Company publications also contribute to these or similar objectives:

1. *Teaching Culture: Strategies for International Communication,* H. Ned Seelye, discusses the development of cultural skills and describes the process by which we acquire cultural traits. This was the first book to focus entirely on the methodology involved in teaching cultural concepts in communications classes.

2. *A TESOL Professional Anthology: Culture,* eleven articles discuss various issues having to do with cross-cultural communication and adaptation, issues that, unless understood by the ESL/EFL instructor, may hinder students' success in the classroom and in English.

3. *101 American Idioms,* by Harry Collis, helps students learn the difference between what Americans sometimes say and what they really mean.

4. *Time: We the People,* readings from *Time* magazine selected by Linda Schinke–Llano, Ph.D., cover a range of cultural topics and develop reading, writing, and oral skills.

How to Use This Book

The mini-dramas in this book involve foreign visitors to the United States and Canada interacting with English-speaking North Americans from varied cultural backgrounds. Characters of many ages and social backgrounds are included, and the various physical settings found in North American are represented: urban, suburban, and rural.

Living in another country can be full of surprises and unexpected problems. This book will help you deal with those surprises and problems. These cross-cultural mini-dramas explore various ways of life that may be different in North America from the way they are in other countries and cultures. Each mini-drama involves one of these differences.

After reading or listening to the dialogue, you are asked to decide the reason for the difference.

1. First, a question is asked, followed by four possible solutions. There may be truth in more than one answer. Some answers may be partly correct.

2. You then decide on the best possible answer to the question.

3. After choosing a solution, you then turn to the page indicated and read the follow-up explanation. It will detail why the answer is right and give further information; or

4. If it is the wrong answer, it will explain why. Often the follow-up explanation will give you a clue so that you can go back and choose the correct solution.

When you travel to North America, knowing about some of the cultural differences will help you better understand your English-speaking friends and associates. If "mini-dramas" occur in your life, you can think up several possible explanations for each situation and have an interesting time discovering the real answer.

1. Sunday Football

Jorge Gutierrez, from Argentina, is visiting his friend Howard Sloan in Washington, D.C. It is early in December.

Howard: Jorge, since this is Sunday, I hope you don't mind if we watch a football game on TV.

Jorge: Not at all, Howie. I've been looking forward to watching one of your football games. As you know, football is an entirely different sport in my country.

Howard: Soccer! I know. More and more North Americans are learning to play soccer. It's fast, rough, and very exciting.

Jorge: You'll have to explain the rules of football to me. I want to be able to follow the game.

Howard: I'll do my best. Pass me the sports section of the newspaper, will you? The *Post* should have the time the game starts. I don't want to miss the kickoff.°

Jorge: Let me see if I can find it. Here it is, on the second page. It says "Washington versus Dallas, 1 P.M., on Channel 9." Does that sound right?

Howard: Yes. Games usually start at one or four o'clock Sunday afternoon. Of course, that's in the East. On the West Coast, the times are three hours earlier.

Jorge: So in California they have to watch the one o'clock game at ten o'clock in the morning.

Howard: Diehard° football fans will watch at any hour. Well, we'd better go out to the store to get some snacks. We want to be ready to see the Cowboys and the Redskins fight it out.

At this point, Jorge is confused. Why?

A. He thinks no one will watch TV that early in the day. (Turn to p. 55)
B. He thinks Howard has changed his mind and wants to watch a Western. (Turn to p. 94)
C. He thinks he's going to watch a soccer match. (Turn to p. 81)
D. Sports fans in Latin America don't serve snacks while watching television. (Turn to p. 68)

---

kickoff: the start of a North American football game, when one team kicks the ball to the other
diehard: very enthusiastic and loyal

2. One of the Family

Wally Witkowski, from Poland, is living with the Gransee family in Boston while he studies English at a local university. The scene is at the dinner table in the dining room.

Wally: That was a wonderful meal. I've never had beef cooked that way.

Marsha: Thanks, Wally. That was Yankee pot roast. It's my grandmother's recipe. She used to serve this meal when we visited her on Sundays. It was a family tradition.

David: And the leftovers° will be good tomorrow and the next day.

Wally: It was delicious, Mrs. Gransee.

Marsha: Please, call me Marsha. If you were a guest who was just going to be here for a day or so, we might be more formal. But you're a part of this family as long as you're here—for both the fun and the work.

Wally: You mean, because I'm living here, I take part in your family traditions?

Marsha: (Laughing) Just like everyone else. Right, Dave?

David: (He rises.) Right. So let's get started, Wally.

What does David expect Wally to do?

A. He expects Wally to join him in a traditional after-dinner game. (Turn to p. 56)
B. He thinks Wally should learn to prepare Yankee pot roast. (Turn to p. 95)
C. He wants Wally to call him by his first name. (Turn to p. 82)
D. He assumes Wally will help him clear the table and do the dishes. (Turn to p. 69)

---

leftovers: food remaining uneaten after a meal

3. Everyday Meals

Wally Witkowski is discussing meals with Marsha and David Gransee. He has been in the United States for only two days.

Wally: I want you to know how much I appreciate these terrific meals you've been cooking. Do you guys° always eat this well?

David: Not really. During the week, we're both busy with our jobs, so there isn't much time to cook anything fancy.

Marsha: We both enjoy cooking and experimenting, so we usually try to fix something special on Sundays.

Wally: This morning's breakfast was great: scrambled eggs, bacon, toast, and orange juice! You surely don't eat that kind of breakfast every day.

Marsha: You're right! We don't. During the week, we usually have cold cereal and maybe a piece of fruit. Neither of us has the time to cook breakfast. Monday through Friday, it's "Every man for himself." Don't worry, though. You'll never go to bed hungry.

David: That's true. And dinners are different, anyway. Some nights Marsha will cook a casserole° or pasta dish. Other nights, I like to throw fish or hamburgers into the broiler and toss a green salad.

Wally: So, you cook every night?

Marsha: Well, not every night. Some nights we have leftovers, or maybe we'll just send out for a pizza. We even enjoy going out to a restaurant once in a while.

How would you describe meals at the Gransee home?

A. They're fixed according to a rigid schedule. (Turn to p. 57)
B. They vary from day to day. (Turn to p. 96)
C. There are no regular mealtimes. (Turn to p. 83)
D. There's usually not much food in the house. (Turn to p. 70)

---

guys: people (informal)
casserole: a combination of foods baked and served in a covered dish

4. Wine with Dinner

Jean Roncin, from a village outside Paris, is visiting his friend Kirk Raab in San Francisco. Jean and his nephew Claude have just arrived for dinner at Kirk's apartment.

Kirk:	Jean, come in. I haven't seen you in weeks. This must be your nephew.
Jean:	Yes, it is. He's spending the summer with me. Claude, say hello to Mr. Raab.
Claude:	How do you do, Mr. Raab. Excuse me, sir. Are we going to eat soon?
Jean:	Claude! Where are your manners? It's not polite to ask for food.
Kirk:	Don't worry, my friend. I understand. I was twelve years old once, and I remember that I was always hungry. Dinner will be ready very soon.
Jean:	What can I do to help?
Kirk:	You could run down to the store to get us a bottle of wine. I completely forgot. I think a dry white wine would be nice with this meal.
Jean:	(He hands Claude some money.) Here, this will keep you occupied until dinner. Go down to the corner and get the wine. (To Kirk) He always does this at home.
Kirk:	Jean, you'd better go with him.

Why can't Claude go to the store alone?

A. Kirk doesn't trust the young boy to buy the right wine.
   (Turn to p. 58)
B. He's in an unfamiliar neighborhood and may get lost.
   (Turn to p. 97)
C. Kirk wants the extra time alone to prepare dinner. (Turn to p. 84)
D. The store will not sell Claude the wine. (Turn to p. 71)

5. Independence Day

Paco Morales, from Mexico City, is visiting his cousin Estela in Los Angeles. It is the Fourth of July, and Estela is describing the planned celebrations.

Paco: I'm looking forward to your Independence Day celebration, Estela. I hear it's a lot of fun.

Estela: Haven't you ever been to one? Don't you have a Fourth of July in Mexico?

Paco: Sure we do. It's the day between the third and the fifth of July. But it's not our Independence Day. That's September sixteenth.

Estela: How silly of me! Of course your day would be different from ours. How do you celebrate on that day?

Paco: Oh, our celebrations are wonderful! We have picnics, we play different sports, some of us go to the beach, and our politicians make speeches.

Estela: Then you'll feel right at home today. That's exactly what we do. I really enjoy the sports in the afternoon. I'm on a softball° team. At the park where we're having our picnic, there are also some volleyball nets.

Paco: How about food? Will there be anything good to eat?

Estela: Sure! We'll barbecue hot dogs and hamburgers and have potato salad, too. I may fry some chicken to bring with us. Also, someone usually brings a watermelon. We'd better get started. I'm hungry just thinking about all that food.

Paco: I've heard that the evening celebration is noisy. Is that true?

Estela: You'll see.

What does Paco expect?

A. He doesn't know; he's never been in the United States before. (Turn to p. 59)
B. He anticipates a fireworks display. (Turn to p. 98)
C. He hopes that the evening meal will be special. (Turn to p. 85)
D. He doesn't think he will like the crowds and noise. (Turn to p. 72)

---

softball: a game similar to baseball

6. What's On?

Nobuo Sako and his wife Mieko, from Japan, are traveling across the United States. They are in a motel room in New York.

Mieko: I'm tired. I hope there are some interesting shows on TV tonight.

Nobuo: Hand me the television program section of the newspaper. I'll see what's on. Here's a review° of some of the prime-time shows.

Mieko: Prime-time? What does that mean?

Nobuo: In television jargon° it means a three-hour period during the evening when the best shows are on, usually from seven to ten o'clock or eight to eleven.

Mieko: I guess that's when the largest audience is available to watch, when people are home from work. What's on tonight?

Nobuo: This review recommends a Burt Reynolds movie. Another channel has a baseball game, and the other channels have sitcoms.° Except for the game, it seems everything tonight is a rerun.° I guess summer isn't the season for first-run shows or movies.

Mieko: As you know, I'm not much of a sports fan. Are there any news shows or talk shows on?

Nobuo: Let's see. The news is on from six to seven o'clock and again at eleven. It looks as though the talk shows are all on late. The first one begins at eleven-thirty.

Mieko: Too bad. After this long, tiring day, I'll probably be asleep by ten-thirty. But let's turn the TV on anyway. Maybe something will hold our attention.

What will they watch?

A. They will watch the baseball game. (Turn to p. 60)
B. They will watch the late news and a talk show. (Turn to p. 99)
C. They will watch nothing. They're both too tired to stay awake. (Turn to p. 86)
D. They will watch reruns of old sitcoms or a movie. (Turn to p. 73)

---

review: a critical evaluation of a book, play, TV show, etc.
jargon: the specialized language of a trade or profession
sitcom: short for *situation comedy*, a humorous TV show having standard characters who appear in different stories each week
rerun: a showing of a program after its original showing

7. The Right Way to Drive

Mbele Wasungu, a student from Kenya, is renting a car at the airport so that he can drive to the university, where he will start classes in a few days.

Clerk: (At the car rental counter) Well, Mr. Wasungu, you're all set. You've got your international driver's license, your rental agreement, and the keys to your car. Anything else?

Mbele: Perhaps you could give me a quick review of your driving customs. The traffic signals are the same as in my country, aren't they?

Clerk: I think they're the same all over: green means go; yellow means caution; and red means stop.

Mbele: All right. Thank you. Do you have a local map? I need to find out how to get to the university.

Clerk: Let's see if we can find it on this small map. (They both examine the map.) Oh, this looks easy. When you exit the airport parking lot, you will merge° right with the traffic. Stay on that road for two miles, and then turn left at the third traffic light. There's a left-hand turn lane. You can't miss it. You'll be all right.

Mbele: Why would I need a special lane to turn left? Is there oncoming traffic at that light?

Why is Mbele confused?

A. He forgot that *right* also means "correct." (Turn to p. 61)
B. He has never driven in the United States. (Turn to p. 100)
C. He's used to driving on the left-hand side of the road. (Turn to p. 87)
D. In the United States, most people are left-handed. (Turn to p. 74)

---

merge: to join

8. Starting High School

Nguyen Thieu is nervous as he talks to other students about his classes. It is morning, and they are walking to school.

Nguyen: Chuck, why are we called freshmen?
Chuck: I don't know. A freshman is what a student in his or her first year of high school is called.
Mary: It's probably because we're fresh and new starting at this school. Speaking of starting, what did you think of that registration° scene in the auditorium yesterday?
Nguyen: It was incredible. I've never seen such confusion.
Mary: My brother is a sophomore, and he says it was even worse last year when he started high school!
Chuck: I can't believe anything could be less orderly, unless it's Mary's desk. What a mess!
Nguyen: You two bicker° like children. Don't you like each other?
Mary: We've always joked with each other, but we don't mean any harm. It's just our way of kidding around.°
Chuck: Yeah. It's a good thing Mary and I aren't in too many classes together. We'd be getting into trouble all the time. But you two are in the same homeroom, aren't you?
Mary: Yes, and we'd better get going.

Where are Mary and Nguyen going?

A. They are going to a classroom where students report daily. (Turn to p. 62)
B. They are going home. Registration takes place the day before school opens. (Turn to p. 101)
C. They are going back to the auditorium to finish registering. (Turn to p. 88)
D. They are going nowhere. Mary is still joking with Chuck. (Turn to p. 75)

---

registration: the act of enrolling in a school or a class
bicker: to quarrel, or argue, about small matters
kid around: to joke, especially with a friend

9. Sandwiches to Go

Two friends at a delicatessen in Buffalo, New York.

Joe: Kim, let's get some sandwiches to go°. We can eat them in the park over by Lake Erie.

Kim: Good idea. But I want to try something different today. The only sandwiches I've had since I arrived are ham-and-cheese and hamburgers.

Joe: Remember those submarine sandwiches I wrote you about? Back in Philadelphia we call them hoagies. This place has a lot of different kinds of subs—mixtures of cold cuts,° cheese, lettuce, tomatoes, onions, hot peppers, and other stuff,° served in a roll that has been cut open. We could try one.

Kim: Those rolls look like miniature submarines. I guess that's where the name comes from. I don't know what kind to order.

Joe: Well, I'm having my favorite—salami and cheese. It also has oil and seasonings and some black olives. It's delicious.

Kim: I don't like olives. I think I'll try a different kind.
(He looks up at the counterman and at the list of items for sale.)

Man: What kind of hero do you want?

What did the man mean?

A. He misunderstood and thought Kim didn't want a sandwich. (Turn to p. 63)
B. Heroes are sandwiches similar to hoagies. (Turn to p. 102)
C. There is only one kind of hoagie. (Turn to p. 89)
D. The delicatessen doesn't serve sandwiches anymore. (Turn to p. 76)

---

to go: to be eaten outside the place where it was bought
cold cuts: assorted slices of cold meats
stuff: things (informal)

10. At the Checkout Counter

In line at the checkout counter of a large, modern supermarket.

Maria: Look at this headline: "Elvis Baby Born on Spacecraft." Where do these tabloids° get such crazy stories?

Iris: I've often wondered the same thing. I also wonder who reads them. Then I realize that I'm standing here reading them myself.

Maria: It looks as though everyone in line reads them, or at least looks at the headlines.

Iris: I think we picked the right line. This one seems to be moving more quickly than the others.

Maria: Maybe our checker is faster at scanning° the food.

Iris: I'm glad. We have only about twenty things here, and I'm in a hurry to get home.

(The customer in front of them pays and leaves.)

Checker: Good afternoon, ladies. Paper or plastic?

Iris: Paper bags, please. You know, yours is the fastest-moving line in the store.

Checker: Well, I'll let it go this time, but in the future, please don't use the express line with so many items.

What did the women do wrong?

A. The checker was telling Iris and Maria to place their purchases up on the conveyer belt more quickly. (Turn to p. 64)

B. Iris and Maria had more than the maximum number of items, so they were in the wrong line. (Turn to p. 103)

C. They missed their chance to read the newspaper headlines that were displayed along another checkout aisle. (Turn to p. 90)

D. They went to a checkout line that was for food items only. (Turn to p. 77)

---

tabloid: a newspaper with small pages, many pictures, and little serious news
scan: to read and record a price electronically

11. Participation in Class

In a sixth-grade math class.

Teacher: Okay, class, please take out your homework. I want to review the answers to the problems you did. Li, what's the answer to number one?
(Li looks down at his paper.)
Teacher: Li, please look up here at me when you're called on. I know you know the answer. Did you do the assignment?
Li: (Shyly) Yes, Ms. Davidson. The answer is thirty-one. I always do my homework.
Teacher: Good. Now remember, I want you to speak up when you know the answer. We're all here to take part in this class.
(Later, after class)
Li: Is Ms. Davidson angry at me? She always seems to pick on° me.
Jack: She's not annoyed. She talks to everybody that way. She wants us to participate in the class and to speak up when we know the answer.
Li: But I don't want to be impolite.
Jack: Don't worry. You're doing fine. You always do the work, and you usually know the answer.

What is Li's problem?

A. He's worried about his schoolwork. (Turn to p. 65)
B. He rarely knows the correct answer. (Turn to p. 104)
C. He's afraid of the teacher, so it's difficult for him to participate in the class. (Turn to p. 91)
D. He doesn't speak and act confidently. (Turn to p. 78)

---

pick on: to criticize or blame

Cultural Encounters in the U.S.A.

12. An Innocent Hug

At a party.

Hans: Dana is such a warm, friendly person. I always love seeing her.
Werner: Me, too. She smiles so easily, and I like the way she hugs° people when she greets them.
Elsa: Well, I don't. Back in my village, a girl doesn't hug a boy unless she's going out with him.
Hans: You're just jealous because she's so popular. If you were friendlier, people would like you better.
Elsa: I'm friendly, and lots of people like me. I listen to my friends, and I care about them. I just don't want boys to get the wrong idea.
Werner: How can you get a wrong idea about something as innocent as a hug? It's a friendly way to greet people. I like it. You should try it.
Elsa: Well, I don't think it's right.

Why does Elsa think Dana shouldn't hug people?

A. She thinks body contact is a romantic or sexual signal. (Turn to p. 66)
B. She thinks boys and girls should never hug each other. (Turn to p. 105)
C. She's jealous of Dana. (Turn to p. 92)
D. She's wary, or careful, of any activity she doesn't understand. (Turn to p. 79)

---

hug: to hold closely in one's arms, a sign of affection

13. Private Thoughts

At a health and fitness center in New York City.

Jorge: Steve seems unusually quiet today. I guess he doesn't like losing at racquetball°.
Mac: It's more than that. Steve has personal problems.
Jorge: Well, they're keeping him from concentrating on his game. Today he played worse than last week. This is a new sport for me, but I beat him three games out of five.
Mac: You're right. He usually plays much better. I think he has problems at home . . . you know, with his wife. I've asked him about his marital difficulties, but he doesn't like to talk about it. I wish he knew it was okay to talk about his problems.
(Steve enters the room.)
Mac: Hi, Steve. Good game.
Steve: Thanks, Mac.
Jorge: Actually, it wasn't so good. You missed a lot of shots. What's worrying you, Steve?
Steve: Did you guys see the baseball game on TV last night? What a game! You know, Jorge, we'll get you hooked° on baseball in no time.

Why didn't Steve answer Jorge's question?

A. He objected to Jorge's telling him he didn't play well. (Turn to p. 67)
B. He's more interested in baseball than in racquetball.
(Turn to p. 106)
C. He felt uncomfortable discussing a very personal problem.
(Turn to p. 93)
D. Men never discuss their feelings. (Turn to p. 80)

---

racquetball: a game similar to tennis, played in a four-walled court
hooked: having a great liking for and very often using, doing, watching, etc.

14. Here Comes the Bride

At a wedding reception in St. Louis, Missouri.

Kim: Thanks for inviting me to your friend's wedding. I was surprised to hear the bride° and groom° talking to each other that way during the marriage ceremony. Is that common?

Sam: Well, some people use a standard set of words, but many couples today write their own wedding vows.°

Kim: Your tradition of throwing rice as they got into their car was fun, but it didn't look like real rice to me.

Sam: It wasn't. It was birdseed. We don't throw rice anymore because someone discovered that birds come along and eat the rice and have trouble digesting it.

Kim: Oh, I didn't think of that. Well, this reception reminds me of wedding parties back in Korea. Plenty of food and drink, music and dancing, and interesting traditions.

Sam: Wait until you see what happens next! The bride is getting ready to throw her bouquet.° Let's go over and watch.

Kim: She's got quite a crowd around her. Oh, look! That little girl caught it!

Sam: She's my friend's ten-year-old niece. I guess there won't be another wedding in this family for a long time.

What does Sam mean?

A. Weddings are expensive. It would be difficult for a family to afford more than one every few years. (Turn to p. 68)
B. The little girl is too young to be the next one married. (Turn to p. 55)
C. He disapproved of the couple's writing their own wedding vows. (Turn to p. 94)
D. It's bad luck for a child to catch the bride's bouquet. (Turn to p. 81)

---

bride: a woman about to be married or just married **vow:** a promise
groom: a man about to be married or just married **bouquet:** a bunch of flowers

14 *Cultural Encounters in the U.S.A.*

15. Strong Coffee

Five A.M. in Miami, Florida.

John: Are you ready, Ali?
Ali: I'm ready, but I'm not fully awake yet. Are you sure we have to get up this early to catch fish?
John: Yes, I'm positive. I've been doing this for years. If we get out on the water before the sun comes up, we'll have the best luck. Trust me.
Ali: Well, I'm glad you're driving. My eyes are still half closed.
John: It's hard for me to wake up sometimes, too. I usually rely on some strong coffee to help me.
Ali: That's what I do at home. We drink a lot of coffee in my family. Why don't I brew° some? We can take it with us.
John: No. Let's get on the road. We can stop along the way.
Ali: I thought you were eager° to get to the lake before the sun comes up.

What does John have in mind?

A. He plans to stop at a restaurant and have breakfast. (Turn to p. 69)
B. He plans to skip coffee this morning. (Turn to p. 56)
C. He plans to stop at a convenience store.° (Turn to p. 95)
D. He wants to let Ali know that he doesn't enjoy brewed coffee. (Turn to p. 82)

---

brew: to mix with hot water and prepare for drinking
eager: full of interest
convenience store: a small supermarket with long hours and short lines

16. Dinner at Eight

Chan Lee, a visiting professor at Yale, is in Ted and Ella Lewis's apartment. She arrived from China a month ago.

Chan: Thanks for offering to give me a lift.° I'm looking forward to this party, but I didn't want to go alone.
Ella: Don't mention it. It's our pleasure. Have you been to one of these large, sit-down dinner parties since you got to New Haven?
Chan: No, this is my first. Last week I went to a cookout° for new professors at Dean Barksdale's home. I took a taxi because I didn't want to be late. But I was the first one there.
Ted: I'll bet you were a little embarrassed.
Chan: You're right. The invitation said "two to seven." I was there at two o'clock, but most people didn't arrive until three or four. They didn't start cooking until five o'clock.
Ted: Cookouts often start slowly. A two o'clock start means you arrive any time after two. (To his wife) Are you ready yet, dear?
Ella: Almost. I was late getting back from the mall, but I'm hurrying.
Chan: Why are you in such a hurry? They said, "Dinner at eight," and it's only seven-fifteen. I don't want to be the first one there again.
Ted: Don't worry. We won't be the first.

Why is Ella hurrying?

A. She wants Chan to get to the party early. (Turn to p. 70)
B. People who arrive early at dinner parties can leave early. (Turn to p. 57)
C. Dinner-party guests usually arrive an hour early. She's already late. (Turn to p. 96)
D. Guests will sit down at the table at eight o'clock, so she doesn't want to arrive late. (Turn to p. 83)

---

lift: a ride
cookout: an informal meal cooked and eaten outdoors

16 *Cultural Encounters in the U.S.A.*

17. Just Call Me Erica

Abile Kimilili, an African exchange student, is touring a radio station in Minneapolis.

Erica: Welcome to America, Abile. How's it going? I'm Erica Kay, the station manager.
Abile: How do you do, Madam Erica. Thank you for showing me around your station. I'm going to study radio broadcasting at the University of Minnesota. I look forward to meeting your staff.
Erica: They're a fine group. We're pretty informal around here, so why don't you start by dropping the "Madam." Just call me Erica.
(A man enters the room.)
Erica: Hey, Fred! How's it going? Glad you're back from vacation. We missed you around here.
Fred: Erica! How are you doing, girl? (He slaps Erica's open palm with his palm.)
Erica: (She laughs.) You turkey.° You're half an hour late on your first day back.
Fred: Who is this dude?°
Erica: Shake hands with Abile. He's from Senegal.
Fred: What's happening, my man?
Abile: I'm visiting your station.

Why is Abile's response inappropriate?

A. Abile thought a standard informal greeting was actually a question. (Turn to p. 71)
B. He thought Fred was referring to his lateness. (Turn to p. 58)
C. He should have asked Fred what was happening. (Turn to p. 97)
D. He thought he should include Erica in the conversation. (Turn to p. 84)

---

turkey: a bird, but in this context a friendly expression meaning "foolish person"
dude: man (informal)

18. Bargain Hunting

Saturday morning in Atlanta.

Soong: Why are you reading the classifieds?° What do you need?
David: I'm looking for a bookcase, but I don't want to buy a new one.
Soong: Are you having any luck?
David: Not really. There aren't any used bookcases listed. But there are a few rummage sales° on Saturday. I think I'll go to them.
Soong: Do you mind if I go with you?
David: Not at all. These private sales are great places to bargain. And sometimes you can find terrific things among all the junk.°
Soong: I learned to negotiate from my mother. I thought I was pretty good at bargaining, but I had a problem the other day at Kimble's Department Store.
David: What happened?
Soong: I wanted to buy a beautiful wool sweater for my girlfriend. It was priced at forty dollars, so I started by offering the salesclerk thirty.

What was Soong's problem?

A. He needs to learn how to bargain at American-style rummage sales. (Turn to p. 72)
B. His offer of thirty dollars for a forty-dollar sweater was an insult. (Turn to p. 59)
C. He was bargaining in the wrong place. (Turn to p. 98)
D. Bargain hunters shop only at rummage sales. (Turn to p. 85)

---

classified: a small advertisement in a newspaper by a person who wants to buy or sell something, offer or get a job, etc.
rummage sale: a sale of used clothing and other things, often for a good cause such as helping the poor
junk: old, useless things

18 *Cultural Encounters in the U.S.A.*

19. How Much Should I Leave?

Several Japanese businessmen are unpacking in their San Diego hotel room.

Suji: Did you tip the bellboy?°
Takashi: Yes, but I don't think it was enough. He looked disappointed. I gave him three dollars.
Tetsuo: That sounds about right to me, fifty cents a bag. If they think you don't know better, they'll try to get more.
Suji: It's the same in Tokyo. But I definitely think we overtipped the cab driver. The fare was twenty dollars, and you gave him a five-dollar tip. That's twenty-five percent of the total! Too much!
Takashi: I disagree. He was polite and informative, and he drove smoothly. One should reward good service.
(Later in the hotel dining room)
Tetsuo: I'll sign for dinner and charge it to our room. Let's see. The bill is one hundred dollars. That seems reasonable. How much tip should I leave?
Suji: Remember last month when we were in Europe? Maybe Californians use that same system: they add the waiter or waitress's tip into the bill, so you don't have to leave anything extra.

Is Suji right?

A. Yes. A tip of fifteen percent is added to every restaurant bill. (Turn to p. 73)
B. No. Restaurant customers are expected to tip the waiter, the bartender, and the busboy°, individually. (Turn to p. 60)
C. No. The average tip is fifteen to twenty percent, depending on the service. (Turn to p. 99)
D. No. There is no standard tipping policy in the United States. (Turn to p. 86)

---

bellboy: a hotel employee who carries luggage; also bellhop, or bellman
busboy: a restaurant employee who clears tables, brings water, etc.

20. Proud of Their Heritage

Rajib Punja is an Indian° medical student at Johns Hopkins University.

Rajib: What are we doing this weekend?
Theo: I'd like to take you to an Italian festival at the Inner Harbor. Every weekend during the summer, a different Baltimore ethnic group takes over the harbor area. It's great fun.
Rajib: Is there an Indian weekend?
Theo: No, I don't think so. There aren't that many Indians in this part of the country, I guess. The largest ethnic groups in Baltimore—after African-Americans—are Hispanics, Italians, and Irish.
Rajib: I've noticed quite a few signs in German, too.
Theo: Yes. People here are proud of their heritage. At the harbor festivals, you get to taste that group's foods, hear their music, and buy traditional things from their country. Last week I bought some fantastic kielbasa sausage at the Polish festival.
Rajib: Which is your favorite festival?
Theo: Well, my wife likes the Dutch° festival because she's part Dutch and part English. But I guess I like the Greek festival because my parents are from Greece.
Rajib: But I thought you both were Americans.

Why is Rajib confused?

A. He's worried that there are so many foreigners living in Baltimore. (Turn to p. 74)
B. Many Americans, especially those in large Eastern cities, refer to themselves ethnically. (Turn to p. 61)
C. Theo doesn't look Greek. (Turn to p. 100)
D. He wasn't aware of the widespread ethnic and cultural diversity in the United States. (Turn to p. 87)

Indian: refers to people from India (Some use the term to mean Native American.)
Dutch: refers to people from Holland (the Netherlands)

21. A Riddle

Mario and Maria are surprised by some of their assumptions.

Debbie: You're more than just brother and sister, aren't you?
Maria: Yes, we're twins.° I was born first, and my brother came a few minutes later. Mama says it's because I'm a girl, and girls should go first.
Mario: I let her go first. Italian boys are always polite. You know, we've been very close all our lives.
Debbie: Well, I have a riddle° for you to solve together.
Mario: I love riddles!
Debbie: A boy and his father were badly injured when the car they were riding in was struck by a truck. The child needed an immediate operation. He was wheeled into the operating room. The surgeon entered and said, "I can't operate on this child—he's my son."
Maria: How can that be? Didn't you say the father was badly injured? How could he possibly operate?
Debbie: Yes, the father's injuries were quite serious.
Mario: Maybe the surgeon was his stepfather.°
Debbie: Nice try, but that's not it.
Mario: Well, I give up.°
Maria: Me, too. What's the answer?
Debbie: What are you both assuming that is keeping you from solving the riddle?

What assumption is keeping Mario and Maria from solving the riddle?

A. They are assuming that the father wasn't hurt too badly in the accident. (Turn to p. 75)
B. They are assuming that surgeons would not operate on their own children. (Turn to p. 63)
C. They are assuming that there could be no answer to the riddle. (Turn to p. 102)
D. They are assuming that the father was the surgeon. (Turn to p. 88)

---

twins: two children born of the same mother at the same time
riddle: a difficult and amusing question to which one must guess the answer
stepfather: the husband of one's mother after the death or divorce of the father
give up: to stop working at or trying to do something

22. Traveling by Train

Mahmoud, from Iran, is on a train in the Midwest.

Mahmoud: (To a passing conductor) Excuse me. Is this Amtrak° schedule correct? Will we arrive in Chicago at three-thirty?
Conductor: You got it. (The conductor walks away.)
Mahmoud: (To a woman sitting beside him) I got what?
Passenger: You've got the correct information. It's a short way of saying "you're correct."
Mahmoud: I see. I studied English in Iran, but some of the idioms° and pronunciation are still difficult for me.
Passenger: Is this your first trip to the Windy City?
Mahmoud: I beg your pardon?
Passenger: Chicago. I think they call it that because there's so much wind.
Mahmoud: Yes, it's my first trip. I'm touring the country by train. The U.S. countryside is beautiful.
Passenger: It certainly is, especially in my neck of the woods.° I'm from Alabama. Do you all plan to travel down that way?
Mahmoud: I'm traveling alone.

Why did Mahmoud say he was traveling alone?

A. He thought the woman wanted him to travel with her. (Turn to p. 76)
B. He thought she was using a plural pronoun. (Turn to p. 63)
C. He wondered why she was talking about her neck. (Turn to p. 102)
D. He thought he was on the wrong train. (Turn to p. 89)

Amtrak: a major train system in the United States
idiom: a phrase having a special meaning
neck of the woods: an area or part of the country (informal)

23. How Cold Is It?

Benigno, from the Philippines, is on a snowy Denver street in January.

Benigno: Harry, this is the coldest place I've ever visited. Does it ever get warm here?

Harry: Every summer. Spring in the Rocky Mountains is also a beautiful time of the year. Too bad your company didn't send you here a few months later, say in April or May.

Benigno: I've never seen this much snow before.

Harry: Winter is long, cold, and wet in Colorado. The snows start around late October and continue through March, at least.

Benigno: People warned me it was cold in many parts of the States at this time of year, but I never expected this.

Harry: Actually, this isn't so bad. Last week we had a real cold spell.° The temperature got down to near zero. But this snow will probably melt quickly because the weather report says that later today it might go up to thirty-five degrees.

Benigno: That's great! It will be as hot as Manila. I'll feel right at home.

What did Benigno forget?

A. He forgot his warm clothes. (Turn to p. 77)
B. He forgot that Denver has cold, snowy weather in the winter. (Turn to p. 64)
C. He forgot that temperatures in the United States are still measured on the Fahrenheit scale. (Turn to p. 103)
D. He forgot that Americans are used to cold weather. (Turn to p. 90)

---

cold spell: a short period of very cold temperatures

24. A Birthday on the Beach

A group of friends have gathered on the beach near Honolulu.

Janet: José, I'm glad you made it.° We're planning a party for Andy, and your part is important.
José: What's the occasion?
Janet: He was born thirty years ago this Saturday. I've invited a lot of his friends to help celebrate.
José: Is it the feast of Saint Andrew?
Janet: No, we don't celebrate a person's saint's day, only the anniversary of the day of his or her birth.
José: So, what can I do?
Janet: I want you to ask Andy to take you scuba° diving. You're new to the islands, so he'll go along with it. While you guys are out looking at fish, we'll set up a party on the beach. Come out of the water about two o'clock.
José: What if it rains?
Janet: On this part of the island, it rains only in the morning. The rain is predictable here. It's not like Argentina: here we know when it's going to rain.
José: So, when it's two o'clock, I'll tell him it's time to come out for his birthday party.
Janet: No! Please don't do that.

Why does Janet tell him not to do that?

A. Janet is worried that it might rain on the day of the party. (Turn to p. 78)
B. It's bad luck to talk about birthdays before they happen. (Turn to p. 65)
C. She wants Andy and José to scuba dive longer. (Turn to p. 104)
D. She wants Andy to be surprised when he comes out of the ocean. (Turn to p. 91)

---

make it: to arrive
scuba: an instrument used for breathing while swimming underwater

25. What to Wear

Doris, a journalist for a San Juan newspaper, is attending a conference in New Orleans.

Doris: Gina, I want your advice on something. Some scientists I met at the conference this afternoon have invited me to a party. Actually, they called it an "informal get-together."
Gina: And what's the problem?
Doris: When I asked how people were going to dress, Dr. Lite said it was casual.
Gina: And you want to know what to wear?
Doris: Well, last night I went out with some journalists for a "casual" party, but I was overdressed.° I wore what I consider casual—an outfit° of skirt, blouse, scarf, medium heels . . . you know.
Gina: That sounds just right to me. What was wrong with it?
Doris: Everyone else there was wearing blue jeans. Several of the women had on running shoes. I felt out of place. So I have no idea° what to wear tonight.
Gina: My guess is you can safely wear last night's outfit to tonight's party.

Why does Gina say this?

A. Casual means blue jeans only to journalists. (Turn to p. 79)
B. Scientists have their own special dress code. (Turn to p. 66)
C. Casual means different things to different people. (Turn to p. 105)
D. She thinks tonight's party has a certain dress code. (Turn to p. 92)

---

overdressed: wearing clothes that are too formal
outfit: clothes worn together
have no idea: to be confused about

26. A Traditional Christmas

Lo Fen, a Chinese agronomist,° is staying with the Helms family in Iowa. It's Christmas Eve.

Lo Fen: Your tree looks beautiful. Do you decorate it this way every year?

Mrs. Helms: Yes, it's a family tradition dating back to my childhood. We use the same lights and ornaments, but of course we have a new tree each year.
(She hands him a delicate glass ball.)
The children made some of these decorations. Here, you can hang this on one of those high branches.
(Lo stands on a ladder to reach the upper limbs.)

Mr. Helms: Well, everything seems to be just about ready. Now all we need is snow.

Lo Fen: Do you exchange the presents in the morning?

Mrs. Helms: Oh, yes. The kids are too excited to wait. After we clean up the mess—all the empty boxes and the wrapping paper—we have a big breakfast. Then the kids have the whole day to play with their new toys.

Mr. Helms: And we'll have a great turkey dinner at around four o'clock. My brother and his family will be joining us.

Lo Fen: I look forward to meeting them. Well, it's late, so I'll say good night. I'll see you bright and early tomorrow so I can share your Christmas morning.

Mr. Helms: Good night, and I hope the fat man in the red suit doesn't wake you up!

What is Mr. Helms talking about?

A. He's making an idiomatic reference to the turkey that will be served for Christmas dinner. (Turn to p. 80)

B. It's a Christmas-morning tradition in Iowa for the father in the family to dress up in a red suit. (Turn to p. 67)

C. The imaginary man who brings gifts at Christmas (Santa Claus, Papa Noel, Father Christmas) is often depicted as wearing a red suit. (Turn to p. 106)

D. He is referring to snow: December snowstorms in the Midwest are often noisy. (Turn to p. 93)

---

agronomist: an expert in farming

27. Walking the Dog

Late in the afternoon in Kansas City.

Delfina: Let's walk the dog. He's been in the apartment all day.
Pam: Good idea. Besides, he probably has to go out.
(Pam gets the dog's leash,° and speaks to the animal.) Come on, Chief. Here, boy!
(They leave to walk the dog down the street.)
Delfina: The poor dog! Do you have to keep him tied to that rope? He's such a gentle animal. Can't we let him run free?
Pam: Not in the city: there are leash laws. If we were out in the countryside, he could run. But here he might get hit by a car or trample someone's garden. Also, some people are afraid of dogs.
Delfina: I'm not. In my country, you see dogs running free everywhere. Speaking of dogs, I'm getting hungry. Let's stop in this diner° and get a hot dog or maybe a chili dog.°
Pam: You know, I'm hungry, too. Let's take Chief home and come back here for dinner.

Why did Pam want to take Chief home?

A. Dogs don't eat hot dogs or chili dogs. (Turn to p. 81)
B. Chief was not a Seeing Eye dog.° (Turn to p. 68)
C. Chief didn't have a proper leash. (Turn to p. 55)
D. People in restaurants are afraid of dogs. (Turn to p. 94)

---

leash: a rope, chain, or strap tied to a dog's collar to control it **diner:** a small restaurant
chili dog: a hot dog sandwich with chili peppers and tomato sauce
Seeing Eye dog: a dog trained to lead a blind person

Cultural Encounters in the U.S.A.   27

28. All You Can Eat

Rosa is a Spanish exchange student who is visiting her friend in Toronto.

Tony: Want to send out for some Chinese?
Rosa: Some what?
Tony: Some Chinese food. I'm hungry, and there's a take-out restaurant near here. We can have them deliver and then watch the news on TV while we eat.
Rosa: No, I'd rather go out. What about that all-you-can-eat place we passed the other day, the one over in the shopping center?
Tony: Okay. I could get up for° that. It's called Al's Steakhouse. They also have great fried fish, and I love their salad bar.° You can go back to refill your plate as often as you like.
Rosa: Is that the place that serves such large portions of meat?
Tony: Yes, their steaks are enormous. Sometimes I can't finish what I've ordered.
Rosa: What if that happens to me? I hate to let food go to waste.
Tony: Don't worry. We'll just get a doggie bag.

What is Tony suggesting?

A. He wants to take any leftover food home to his dog. (Turn to p. 82)
B. He thinks Rosa should order only the salad bar. (Turn to p. 69)
C. He wants to stay home and order some Chinese food. (Turn to p. 56)
D. He wants Rosa to know that the food will not be wasted. (Turn to p. 95)

---

get up for: to become enthusiastic about
salad bar: a table from which diners help themselves to fruits, vegetables, and other foods

29. I Need This Vacation

At a research laboratory in Southern California.

Singh: Anita, I've been here only three days and you're leaving already.
Anita: Just for a few weeks. I need this vacation. You'll be all right. You know the project we're working on, and you're a good scientist. Don't worry. I'll be back as soon as I spend or gamble° all my money.
Singh: Gambling? Where?
Anita: Las Vegas. I find gambling relaxing. I don't take it seriously, the way some people do. Besides, I love the shows and the all-night atmosphere of the town. The casinos° never close, you know.
Singh: (Laughing) If you gamble all night, you'll run out of money in a few days.
(The director of the laboratory walks in.)
Anita: Good afternoon, Dr. Green. I just finished showing Singh the ropes° around here.
Green: That's good. He'll be able to keep the project going in your absence. Where are you going on your vacation?
Anita: I'm going to Nevada to relax. The desert is a good place to get away from the stress of work.
Green: Enjoy yourself. We'll see you when you get back.

Why did Anita tell her boss and her coworker two different versions of her plans?

A. She didn't think Singh knew enough to work without her. (Turn to p. 83)
B. It was a natural reaction. Scientists usually keep their projects secret. (Turn to p. 70)
C. She had to hide her plans to gamble, because it's against the law. (Turn to p. 57)
D. She was reluctant, or unwilling, to tell Dr. Green that she enjoys gambling. (Turn to p. 96)

---

gamble: to risk one's money on horse races, in games, etc.
casino: a building used for playing games for money
show the ropes: to teach someone the rules and customs of a place or activity

30. Nicknames

Lamchul Adiprachan, from Thailand, is being introduced to Bo's friends at a country music bar in Texas.

Bo: Hey, you guys! I want you to meet Lamchul Adiprachan. He's here from Bangkok for a few months to study how we drill oil wells.

Red: (Shaking Adiprachan's hand) Pull up a chair, Lam, and let me get you a beer. It's nice to meet you. Sis, say hello to Lam.

Sis: (Several people stand up to shake Adiprachan's hand.) Hi, Lam.

Lam: Bo, Red, Sis—I've never heard these names before. My English books are full of names like Robert, Patricia, Jennifer, and Michael.

Red: Well, around here we mostly use nicknames.° I came by mine naturally. I don't know if you can tell through all this gray, but my hair used to be red.

Sis: My brother Bo named me when I was little. And his full name is Beauregard.

Lam: So you're his sister. I get it.

Why are the oil drillers calling Lamchul Adiprachan, Lam?

A. They're showing him that he's welcome and accepted. (Turn to p. 84)
B. It's an American custom never to use a person's full name. (Turn to p. 71)
C. All Texans have one-syllable names. (Turn to p. 58)
D. Many Thai names are difficult for Americans to pronounce. (Turn to p. 97)

---

nickname: a name used informally instead of someone's own name

30 *Cultural Encounters in the U.S.A.*

31. A Death in the Family

Nan Kreck's mother has recently died. Nan's English students have come to her mother's wake.°

Rajib: Ms. Kreck, I came to pay my respects° and to offer my sympathy.
Nan: Thank you, Rajib. That's very kind of you. My mother lived a long and happy life. And she was well loved.
Chou: You must be filled with grief over her loss. How can you be so calm?
Nan: My brother and I were lucky to have her as our mother. We cherish her memory.
Louisa: If I lost my mother, I don't know what I'd do. I think I'd completely fall apart.°
Nan: Well, I feel very sad, of course, and I'm going to miss my mom a lot. But I'm also glad she won't have to suffer from her illness° anymore. Now she won't have any more pain.
Laura: But what about your pain, Ms. Kreck? How will you cope° with your sorrow?
Nan: I'm grateful she was my mother—that thought helps me a lot.
Su Lin: Well, I think you're holding up° very well.

Which of these expressions would be best to say to Nan?

A. I'm sorry for your loss. (Turn to p. 85)
B. You poor woman! You must be so sad. (Turn to p. 72)
C. Too bad about your mom. (Turn to p. 59)
D. You must be happy that your mother is no longer in pain. (Turn to p. 98)

---

wake: a gathering to watch and grieve over a dead person on the night before the burial
pay one's respects: to offer sympathy to one in grief over another's death
fall apart: to become unable to control one's feelings of sadness
illness: a sickness
cope: to deal successfully with something
hold up: to survive, endure

32. Really?

Juan, a Costa Rican high school exchange student, is going to live with an American family in Fredericksburg, Virginia.

Diane: I hope you'll be happy here, Juan. You seem like such a friendly, outgoing° person. I'm sure you won't have any trouble making friends.
Juan: Thank you, Mrs. Mullen. I hope you're right.
Bill: Your English is better than I expected. I'll bet you got fantastic grades in language class, didn't you?
Juan: Well, they weren't fantastic, but they were good. I have much more to learn before I sound like a Virginian.
Diane: Your accent is perfect just the way it is! I enjoy the inflection° you give to different words.
Juan: Thank you.
Bill: Here comes our son, James. You'll be sharing a room with him.
James: Hi! You must be Juan. (He shakes Juan's hand.) Glad to meet you. That's a terrific jacket you're wearing.
Juan: Thanks. I got it in San José before I left.
James: That's probably the nicest jacket I've ever seen.
Juan: Really? The nicest?

Why is Juan surprised?

A. He can't believe that they enjoy his Costa Rican accent. (Turn to p. 86)
B. He isn't used to compliments. (Turn to p. 73)
C. He wonders if James wants to borrow his jacket. (Turn to p. 60)
D. He interpreted an exaggeration literally.° (Turn to p. 99)

---

outgoing: showing eagerness to mix socially with others
inflection: a change in the voice according to the needs of expression
literally: according to the words and not the intention

32 *Cultural Encounters in the U.S.A.*

33. Is It a Date?

Juan has been in high school in the United States for two weeks.

Linda:	Hi, Juan. Remember me? I'm in your math class second period.°
Juan:	(Blushing°) Sure, I recognize you. You sit in the front desk of the third row.
Linda:	You always know the answers to the math problems. You're pretty smart.
Juan:	Thanks. I've always been good with numbers. (He hesitates.) Did you know that your name means "pretty" in Spanish? You are, too.
Linda:	Thank you. I'm flattered.° Listen, a bunch of us kids are getting together at Dana's house on Friday evening. Want to come along? We're all meeting at my house at seven o'clock. We'll walk over to Dana's together.
Juan:	I'd love to.
	(Later, Juan is alone with James.)
Juan:	I've been invited to a party Friday night.
James:	Great! I knew it wouldn't take long for you to make friends. Do you have a date?°
Juan:	I'm not sure. Linda, a girl in my math class, invited me, but I don't know if I'm her date.

Does Juan have a date with Linda for the party on Friday night?

A.   No. Girls don't ask boys for dates. (Turn to p. 87)
B.   No. A group of friends are going together. (Turn to p. 74)
C.   Yes. They're going as a couple. (Turn to p. 61)
D.   Yes. Any invitation is considered a date. (Turn to p. 100)

---

period: a division of a school day
blush: to become red in the face, from attention or shame
flatter: to give pleasure to
date: a special social meeting between a man and woman, or boy and girl

34. The Right Size

Alan Garcia, from Peru, is shopping for clothes at a large department store in Tampa, Florida. His wife is with him.

Alan: I hope they have those suits in stock.
Ana: The ones we saw advertised on sale for forty percent off?
Alan: Yes. That's a great price, and I think that style would look good on me.
Clerk: May I help you, sir?
Alan: I'd like to see the gray wool suit that's on sale. Size forty-eight. (The clerk pulls Alan's size from the rack. It is much too large.) I'm swimming in this! I don't understand it. I've been dieting, but I don't think I've lost that much weight.
Ana: (To the clerk) I've been over there looking for dress shirts for my husband, but I can't find his size.
Clerk: We're having size trouble here, too. What's the shirt size you're looking for?
Ana: Thirty-nine.
Clerk: That's going to be a problem!

Why does the clerk say this?

A. The store carries only large-size clothes. (Turn to p. 88)
B. He doesn't know that the Garcias are using a different measuring system. (Turn to p. 75)
C. Alan has lost too much weight to fit into his clothes. (Turn to p. 62)
D. Peruvian men wear smaller sizes than most Florida stores carry. (Turn to p. 101)

35. Sorry I'm Late

A high-school student from Brazil is visiting several American universities with her parents. They are waiting to see the dean° of a small college in Maine.

Father: I see you've brought something to occupy your time while we wait. Good. We may be here a long time.
Isabel: Yes, Papa. I brought the catalog° for the next college we're going to visit—the one in New Hampshire.
Mother: Maybe we won't have to wait long. We've only been here fifteen minutes.
Isabel: I'm not used to the way they treat time here. They wouldn't see me at that place in Massachusetts yesterday. I missed the appointment because I was forty-five minutes late. That's no time at all back in Brasilia.
Father: It's just that North Americans pay more attention to exact times. They're very punctual° people.
Mother: I think that if you're more than thirty minutes late, you have to apologize and explain what delayed° you.
Father: Our appointment with this dean is for three-fifteen. My watch says three-thirty. I'm sure we're not late.
(The dean comes out of his office.)
Dean: Isabel? Come in. Sorry I kept you waiting. We're running a little behind schedule° today.

Which sentence explains the situation?

A. University officers often keep students waiting. (Turn to p. 89)
B. Isabel and her parents are fifteen minutes late for an important appointment. (Turn to p. 76)
C. The dean feels it is unnecessary to explain a short delay. (Turn to p. 63)
D. The dean is apologizing for being late. (Turn to p. 102)

---

dean: an important officer at a college or university
catalog: a book containing useful information
punctual: prompt, on time
delay: to cause to be late
run behind schedule: to do something after the planned time

36. At the Mall

Ana Garcia is visiting her friend, Grace, in Tampa, Florida.

Grace: Come in and have some coffee, Ana. The kids have just gone out to the mall° to hang out° with their friends.
Ana: I saw a lot of teenagers when Alan and I were there yesterday.
Grace: They spend hours there, especially on weekends.
Ana: Speaking of that trip, Alan bought a shirt at a department store, but the sleeves are too long. Do you know a seamstress or tailor who can shorten them?
Grace: I know several. But wouldn't it be easier to take the shirt back and exchange it for the right size?
Ana: Isn't that complicated?
Grace: No, it's easy. We'll just take the shirt back to the men's department and show them the sales slip.° They'll exchange it for the correct size or give you your money back.
Ana: We? Do you want to go with me?
Grace: Sure. I love going to the mall.
Ana: What do you do there—hang out, like the kids?

Why does Grace want to go to the mall?

A. She loves to spend money. (Turn to p. 90)
B. She doesn't really like going to the mall. She just wants to help Ana return her husband's shirt. (Turn to p. 77)
C. She enjoys spending time in a pleasant, socially active place. (Turn to p. 64)
D. She wants to check up on her teenagers. (Turn to p. 103)

---

mall: a large shopping center, often indoors
hang out: to spend time (informal)
sales slip: a receipt given at a store

37. Trick or Treat

Matsuo Kobe is in Phoenix, Arizona, on October 31.

Sarah: Mom asked me to help Molly with her costume° for tonight. That's why I was sewing in the other room.
Matsuo: What did you make for your sister?
Sarah: A ghost° outfit. I wish she had wanted to dress up like something a little more original. Half the little kids on the street tonight will be wearing sheets.
Matsuo: I saw some masks° with horrible faces in a store today. Do the children ever scare anyone?
Sarah: Mostly each other. They're too young to understand the background of Halloween. The legend is filled with ghosts and other scary things, but the evening is really a celebration of life over death, or dead beings.
Matsuo: So dressing up is just symbolic—a way to have some fun?
Sarah: Yes. The kids love to put on costumes and go from door to door, collecting bags of goodies.°
Matsuo: Here come our first visitors now. (Children appear at the door and shout "Trick° or treat!°")

Why do children say "Trick or treat" on Halloween?

A. They're warning people of ghosts on this scary night. (Turn to p. 91)
B. They want to be invited into a home to receive small treats. (Turn to p. 78)
C. They're offering to do a trick for a treat. (Turn to p. 65)
D. It's a way of asking if people like their costumes. (Turn to p. 104)

---

costume: the clothes typical of a certain period, country, or profession
ghost: the spirit of a dead person, who appears again
mask: a covering for the face to hide or change it
goodies: good things to eat (informal)
trick: something done to deceive or make someone look stupid
treat: something that gives pleasure

38. Getting a Ticket

Two Hispanic tourists are walking to their car on a street in Albuquerque, New Mexico.

Rodolfo: What is that woman doing?
Alfredo: That woman is a traffic officer,° and she's writing you a ticket.° What did you do? Forget to put money in the parking meter?
Rodolfo: Officer, what's the problem?
Officer: You're parked in a No Parking zone. Can't you read? That sign says "No parking or standing from 4 to 6 P.M." It's now four-forty P.M.
(She begins to write in her book of tickets.)
Rodolfo: I think I'll settle this matter right now.
Officer: (Handing Rodolfo the ticket) This infraction° is going to cost you twenty dollars. Please sign this, sir. It is not an admission° of guilt. It simply means you understand what the charge° is.
(Rodolfo opens his wallet and begins to take out some money.)
Please, sir, put that away!

What just happened?

A. Rodolfo wanted to convince the traffic officer that he was innocent because he didn't understand the local parking regulations. (Turn to p. 92)
B. The traffic officer was offering to let Rodolfo go with just a warning this time. (Turn to p. 79)
C. Rodolfo was offering to pay the fine.° (Turn to p. 66)
D. Rodolfo was trying to have the ticket fixed.° (Turn to p. 105)

---

traffic officer: a city employee in charge of enforcing parking laws
ticket: a printed notice of an offense against driving laws
infraction: a violation, or breaking, of a law
admission: a statement saying that something is true
charge: a spoken or written statement blaming a person for breaking the law
fine: an amount of money paid as a punishment
fix: to arrange unfairly or dishonestly

39. The Missing Floor

Some Russian students are spending their summer in Philadelphia, visiting historic sights. They are checking into a hotel.

Boris: We'd like a room with two beds, please.
Clerk: A double? Let's see . . . I can put you in room 1405. It faces the river and has a wonderful view.
Alexi: That will be fine. Since we're going to be fourteen stories° above the ground, I think we should definitely have a room with a view.
(Later, Alexi returns from a walk.)
Alexi: Boris, I saw you sitting out on the balcony° of our room. I could see you from the street.
Boris: That's quite a distance. How could you tell who it was?
Alexi: I recognized your bright red shirt. But there's something strange. We're in room 1405, right? Well, when I saw you on the balcony, I counted upward. I only got to twelve. We're on the twelfth floor.
Boris: No, I'm sure we're on the fourteenth floor. The desk clerk said so.
Alexi: I know! I'll look out the window and count downward.°
(He counts.)
I still say we're only twelve stories up.

What is the confusion about?

A. Alexi shows he's stubborn° by insisting on his count, even though he knows they're on the fourteenth floor. (Turn to p. 93)
B. There is no thirteenth floor in many American hotels. (Turn to p. 80)
C. In the United States, the numbering of stories starts at what other countries call the second floor. (Turn to p. 67)
D. Their hotel is on a mountain and their room is in the back, so it seems as if the third floor is the first story. (Turn to p. 106)

---

story: a floor or level in a building
balcony: a place for people to stand or sit, built out on the upstairs wall of a building
downward: going down
stubborn: determined, with a strong will

40. Many Colors

Some visitors from Greece are touring the Revolutionary War° battlefields at Valley Forge, Pennsylvania.

Spiro: Those American Indians over there are very friendly. The man and I were comparing skin color. We're almost exactly the same, but he describes his color as red. Americans certainly come in many colors.

Melina: I think if you look closely at Native American skin, you'll see a reddish tint.°

Spiro: You know, our tour guide yesterday looked as though he was from China, but he said he was born in California.

Melina: Orientals are referred to as Asian-Americans, and I think their skin color is called yellow. People notice skin color or race quite a lot here. Hispanics are called brown.

Spiro: By the white people, you mean?

Melina: By everyone.

Guide: This is where General George Washington spent the winter with his troops.

Spiro: What about our beautiful, brown tour guide? Her skin reminds me of cinnamon.°

Melina: I think she's black.

What does Melina mean?

A. Greek cinnamon isn't brown; it's black. (Turn to p. 94)
B. Americans don't use the word *brown* to describe skin color. (Turn to p. 81)
C. African-Americans are called black. (Turn to p. 68)
D. Americans refer to brown-skinned people as black. (Turn to p. 55)

Revolutionary War: the war between American colonies and Britain which led to independence; also called the American Revolution
tint: a light coloring
cinnamon: a sweet-smelling powder used for giving a special taste to food

41. Going Dutch

Two friends in line at a movie theater in downtown Cleveland, Ohio.

Ari: Come on, Tara. Let's go up to the window and buy our tickets. The movie is starting in a few minutes.

Tara: We can't push in front of the other people in line. Don't be so impatient. We'll be at the head of the line soon.

Ari: (To the cashier) Two tickets, please. How much is it?
(He holds a twenty-dollar bill in his hand.)

Tara: Oh no, Ari. I didn't mean for you to pay for me when I invited you to go tonight. Let's go dutch.° I'll pay my own way. I insist.
(They enter the theater.)

Ari: I'm looking forward to this film. I read a good review of it in this morning's newspaper.

Tara: Me, too. It will be great to see something light and funny for a change. I'm tired of heavy drama.
(They look for empty seats in the theater.)

Ari: Are these seats okay?

Tara: They're fine, but I can't watch a movie without popcorn.

What did they forget?

A. Ari forgot to tip the usher. (Turn to p. 95)
B. Tara forgot to stop at the concession stand. (Turn to p. 82)
C. They didn't find out what kind of movie it was before paying to see it. (Turn to p. 69)
D. Tara forgot to reimburse° Ari for her ticket. (Turn to p. 56)

---

go dutch: each person pays his or her own expenses at an outing; *also dutch treat*
reimburse: to pay back

42. How Much Do You Make?

An Egyptian businessman is visiting a government trade° official in Washington, D.C., the nation's capital.

Malek: Thank you for showing me your offices, Mr. Becker. I can see why Washington bureaucrats° enjoy their jobs.
Becker: Why do you say that?
Malek: The city is beautiful, the offices are modern and comfortable, and the work is so interesting.
Becker: Many people work for the federal government all their adult lives. Government service can be a rewarding and secure career.
Malek: Do you mean financially rewarding?
Becker: Well, many positions pay salaries that are comparable to those in private industry.
Malek: I've always thought that most bureaucrats are lazy.
Becker: Sometimes that's true, but not usually. Most feds° are honest, hard-working professionals. It's hard to keep highly trained people, so the pay and working conditions have to be attractive.
Malek: How much do you make?
Becker: I'm a GS-15. That's high on the scale of workers, but even a GS-1 is paid a living wage.°

What does Mr. Becker's answer mean?

A. All government employees are well paid. (Turn to p. 96)
B. He doesn't want to answer directly. (Turn to p. 83)
C. Lazy employees are paid the same as hard-working ones. (Turn to p. 70)
D. He earns $15,000 a year. (Turn to p. 57)

---

trade: related to the buying and selling of goods
bureaucrat: a government employee
fed: a federal-government employee
living wage: enough earnings to provide a reasonable level of comfort

43. Table Manners

At a Thanksgiving dinner in Juneau, Alaska. There are fourteen guests at the Wrights' dinner table.

Kwan: There's so much food on the table, I don't know where to begin.
Rachel: Pass your plate down to Chuck, Kwan. He'll put meat on it. He always carves° the turkey.
Chuck: White meat or dark, Kwan?
Kwan: Dark, please. I like the drumstick.°
Chuck: (To his wife) Why don't you start passing the potatoes, honey.
Rachel: You know, Kwan, it's okay to pick up the leg with your fingers. You don't have to cut it from the bone. Around here, we think eating should be easy and fun.
Chuck: And try a little bit of everything. Then you can go back for seconds,° after you see which dishes° you like best.
Kwan: (At the end of the meal) I feel so full, I don't think I could eat another bite. Thank you, Chuck and Rachel, for inviting me to share this delicious meal with you and all your friends.
(Kwan belches° loudly.)
Rachel: Kwan!

What sentence describes the situation?

A. Rachel is angry that Kwan burped. (Turn to p. 97)
B. By tradition, Chuck should have been the first person to belch. (Turn to p. 84)
C. Alaskans don't belch. (Turn to p. 71)
D. Kwan is showing how much he enjoyed and appreciated the meal. (Turn to p. 58)

---

carve: to cut cooked meat into slices
drumstick: the lower part of the leg of a cooked bird
go back for seconds: to help oneself to more food
dish: a prepared food
belch: to burp, expel stomach gas through the mouth

44. Summer Sun

Two Chilean students are visiting a friend at a beach resort° in New Jersey. It is August.

Victor: This beach reminds me of one north of Santiago, except the sun sets° in the west there.
Trish: (She laughs.) It sets in the west here, too. What you mean is that the sun sets over the Pacific Ocean when you're looking west. Here the sun rises° over the Atlantic Ocean, in the east.
Flor: He knew that. He's just being silly.
Victor: I'd like to walk on the boardwalk° later, if that's okay with you two. There are some souvenirs I want to buy.
Flor: You just want to eat some of that great American junk food.° You'd be better off if you stayed here on the blanket and took a nap.°
Victor: Good idea. I always get sleepy at the beach.
Flor: On second thought, we've been here a few hours already. Let's put our street clothes on and go up to the boardwalk.
Victor: That's fine with me. I'm so hungry, I could eat my beach pass.°

Why does Flor want to leave the beach?

A. She's jealous and doesn't want Victor to watch other women in bathing suits. (Turn to p. 98)
B. She's worried that too much sun will be harmful. (Turn to p. 85)
C. She wants to go shopping. (Turn to p. 72)
D. Her beach pass is good for only one day. (Turn to p. 59)

---

resort: a vacation place
set: to go down
rise: to come up
boardwalk: an elevated wooden walkway along a beach or waterfront
junk food: snacks with little nutritional value
nap: a short sleep
beach pass: an admission ticket to a public beach, used by local beach towns as a tax

45. Dressed for the Occasion

Trish and her two Chilean friends decide to visit an amusement park.

Victor: Tell me about this amusement park we're going to.
Trish: It's great. You pay one admission fee, and then you can go on all the rides for free. You can stay all day if you want.
Flor: I'm a little tired after spending half the day on the beach. Maybe we should go back to your apartment and freshen up.° Or we could come back tomorrow morning when we're rested.
Trish: We can stop and rest inside the park anytime we want. There are plenty of places where we can relax—restaurants, benches . . .
Flor: Can we go into a restaurant dressed like this?
Trish: Of course. You look fine. In fact, you're dressed perfectly for the occasion. What are you worried about?
Flor: I think we should change out of these shorts. I'm just not comfortable.

What is bothering Flor?

A. She's too tired to go to the park. (Turn to p. 99)
B. She doesn't want to go into a restaurant wearing shorts. (Turn to p. 86)
C. She thinks the clothes she's wearing are too dirty to wear to the amusement park. (Turn to p. 73)
D. She isn't used to wearing shorts in public places. (Turn to p. 60)

---

freshen up: to feel more comfortable and attractive by washing

46. No Smoking

Kokei is meeting with Koichi, an associate from Tokyo, in Koichi's company on Long Island, New York.

Kokei: Have you got a light,° Koichi?
Koichi: No. I gave up smoking a few months ago. And I'd appreciate it if you would wait until we left the office. The employees voted to make this a smoke-free environment, so there's no lighting up° in the building.
Kokei: That's pretty drastic.°
Koichi: Actually, it's not so odd.° A lot of companies are banning° smoking in the workplace. And everyone in this office is a nonsmoker anyway, so it's not a hardship° for us. Have you tried quitting? It isn't as difficult as I thought it would be.
Kokei: I've tried to quit several times, but never had much luck. Listen, let's gather some of the others and continue our meeting at a restaurant. It's almost time for lunch, and I'm getting hungry. But most of all, I need a cigarette.
Koichi: Well, you'll have to smoke it on the way.

Why will Kokei have to smoke his cigarette on the way?

A. Koichi and his office mates would object to Kokei's smoking at lunch. (Turn to p. 100)
B. Restaurants on Long Island don't permit smoking. (Turn to p. 87)
C. They'll be sitting in a nonsmoking section of the restaurant. (Turn to p. 74)
D. Office rules often extend to the lunch place. (Turn to p. 61)

---

light: something that will set a cigarette burning
light up: to begin to smoke
drastic: strong, sudden, and severe
odd: strange
ban: to forbid
hardship: a difficult condition

47. Designated Driver

Cindy Hawkins has invited her Nigerian friend, Milton Oboye, to a happy hour° after work on Friday.

Brenda: Hey, you guys! Over here! We've been waiting for you.
Cindy: Milton, I want you to meet Brenda and the rest of the crazy people I work with.
Brenda: Sit down, Milton. I'll call the waiter and have him get you a drink. What will you have?
Milton: Thanks, Brenda, but I'll pass.°
Brenda: But this is TGIF time, my friend. It's an American custom.
Milton: TGIF?
Cindy: It means "Thank God It's Friday." People celebrate the end of the workweek by having a few drinks with friends. Last week I had too many, and I got drunk.° A friend had to drive me home. It was awful.
(The waiter comes to their table.)
Waiter: Hello. What may I bring you?
Milton: I'll just have a ginger ale,° please. I might have to drive my friend home.
Waiter: Your soda is on the house.°

Why is Milton's drink free?

A. Designated drivers° drink free in many bars. (Turn to p. 101)
B. Many bars offer free drinks to foreigners. (Turn to p. 88)
C. Bars charge only for alcoholic drinks. (Turn to p. 75)
D. By law, nondrinkers don't have to pay at Friday happy hour. (Turn to p. 62)

---

happy hour: a period in the late afternoon when many bars and restaurants lower the prices of their alcoholic beverages
I'll pass: Skip me; I choose not to participate
drunk: overcome by alcohol, intoxicated
ginger ale: a nonalcoholic soda
on the house: free
designated driver: one person in a group of drinkers who promises not to drink alcoholic beverages in order to drive the rest home safely

Cultural Encounters in the U.S.A. 47

48. The Right to Work

Two young men from Haiti are discussing job opportunities in Detroit, Michigan.

Yves: I've been here for two weeks visiting my brother-in-law. He says the auto plants° are hiring, but you have to belong to the union.° Right now, I don't have enough money to join. I'm broke.°
Henri: That's why I'm headed for the Sunbelt.° Sure, there are jobs up here, but if you don't belong to a union, you can't get anywhere.
Yves: Experience must count for something.
Henri: For some jobs, it does, but that doesn't change the union card requirement.
Yves: That must be true everywhere.
Henri: Not where I'm going. Look at this.
(He shows him a "help wanted" ad.)
Yves: (Reading) "No experience necessary. Will train.° Good benefits. Right-to-work state."
Henri: See what I mean? That's why I'm heading south.

Why is Henri moving to the South?

A. The weather is more suitable for Haitians, who are used to a tropical climate. (Turn to p. 102)
B. There are more jobs available in southern and southwestern states than in northern states. (Turn to p. 89)
C. Most auto-manufacturing jobs have moved to Sunbelt locations. (Turn to p. 76)
D. Right-to-work laws prevent discrimination against nonunion labor. (Turn to p. 63)

---

plant: a factory
union: an association of workers
broke: without money (informal)
Sunbelt: the southern and southwestern states of the United States
train: to give teaching and practice in a profession or skill

49. On the Highway

Two tourists from Belize are driving from Cheyenne, Wyoming, to Yellowstone National Park.

Grady: We've covered quite a bit of ground today. I'm starting to get tired, but I really look forward to seeing the geysers° at the park.

Whyte: Me, too, but I'm glad we stopped in Cheyenne. It reminded me more of Belize City than any other state capital we've seen.

Grady: It also looked like those small towns we drove through in the Midwest—clean, unhurried, and friendly. Wouldn't you say?

Whyte: Yes, but I've had enough of being a tourist and of driving for one day. Want to stop for the night?

Grady: Sure, if you do. Pull into that gas station. I'll ask the mechanic where the next motel is.
(Whyte pulls into a service station.)
Is there a motel nearby?

Mechanic: You bet.° There's one just down the road a piece.° Keep going on the highway. You can't miss it.

Grady: Thanks. (To Whyte) Maybe you'd better let me drive. It might take us a while to get there.

Why does Grady think it might take a while?

A. He has changed his mind. He now wants to drive farther before stopping for the night. (Turn to p. 103)
B. The distance between towns in Wyoming is great. (Turn to p. 90)
C. Westerners tend to make little of° distance. (Turn to p. 77)
D. He thinks the mechanic was putting them on.° (Turn to p. 64)

---

geyser: a natural spring of hot water that from time to time rises suddenly into the air
you bet: certainly, for sure
down the road a piece: not far away (informal)
make little of: to treat as unimportant
put (someone) on: to play a joke on, deceive playfully

50. A Bit Crowded

Raul Bezares, a Uruguayan salesman, and a friend are leaving a private showing of an exhibit at the Chicago Art Institute.

Carla: Did you enjoy the exhibit, Raul?
Raul: Very much. I particularly liked the work of that young artist from Puerto Rico. Some of her works would look wonderful in my study at home.
Carla: I enjoyed it, too, but I felt a bit crowded. More people showed up than they anticipated,° I think.
Raul: I didn't mind that part. Mingling° among all those art lovers was exhilarating.°
Carla: Raul, several of us are going over to the hotel now for dinner. Will you join us?
Raul: I'd love to. Who's going?
Carla: Let's see . . . Sandy, Damian, Dr. Bremer. I think there will be five of us.
Raul: I'll be in charge of finding us a taxi, if you'll round up° the others.
Carla: I think we'll need two cabs.

Why will they probably go in two taxis?

A. Raul will need extra room for the paintings he bought. (Turn to p. 104)
B. Taxis in Chicago are small, holding a maximum of four people. (Turn to p. 91)
C. North Americans tend to spread out, requiring more personal space than people of many other cultures. (Turn to p. 78)
D. Carla will never be able to get all five people together before they leave the museum. (Turn to p. 65)

---

anticipate: to expect
exhilarating: lively, stimulating, enjoyable
mingle: to mix with people
round up: to gather together in one place

51. Stage Fright

Branca, a musician/actor from Angola, is touring western Canada. He is backstage with the local producer of his show.

Colson: Welcome to Vancouver, Branca. You're a long way from home.
Branca: Yes, and I'm a little nervous. This is the first stop on my North American tour.
Colson: Where will you go next?
Branca: I'll visit a few other large cities in the Western Provinces, then head south to Seattle and some college campuses in the Northwest of the United States.
Colson: You've been performing for years, though, haven't you? Why so jittery?°
Branca: I suppose it's the strain of so much travel, the large audiences of foreigners, and the fear that people won't like my songs.
Colson: From what I've heard, you don't have any worries on that last item. Your music and your messages are terrific. I'm sure they'll be well received.°
Branca: Thanks. I hope I don't get so unnerved° that I trip over my lines.
Colson: Well, it's show time. (He slaps Branca on the back.) Break a leg!

What does Colson mean by this?

A. He's trying to break the tension with a joke. (Turn to p. 105)
B. He's using an old show-business way of wishing good luck. (Turn to p. 92)
C. He's teasing Branca about his fear of stumbling, or tripping. (Turn to p. 79)
D. He's showing his jealousy of the singer. (Turn to p. 66)

---

jittery: nervous, uneasy
well received: accepted and appreciated
unnerve: to take away the courage of

52. Seven Years of Bad Luck

Lucy, a Jamaican trainee at the World Bank, is reporting for her first day at work.

May: I'm sorry we're looking so jumbled,° Lucy. We just moved into these new offices. As you can see, everything is a bit messy. And to top it off,° today is Friday the 13th.

Lucy: Maybe I can help you get organized.

May: Good idea. You can start by bringing me that box—the one over against the wall.
(Lucy goes to get the box.)
Be careful! Don't walk under that ladder!

Lucy: Sorry. Here's the box. Shall I put the contents into drawers?

May: Look out! The bottom of the box is about to come open.
(Things spill out of the box. A small mirror falls onto the floor and breaks.)

Lucy: Oops. I'm being a bit clumsy° today.

May: It looks as though we're in for seven years of bad luck.

What does May mean?

A. She wishes her office hadn't moved on this particular date. (Turn to p. 105)

B. She thinks that Lucy has brought bad luck to the organization by walking under a ladder. (Turn to p. 93)

C. She's referring to an old superstition regarding broken mirrors. (Turn to p. 80)

D. She's nervous over the mess and confusion created by the office move. (Turn to p. 67)

---

jumbled: mixed up, in confusion
top it off: to increase something, making it either better or worse
clumsy: awkward and ungraceful in movement

52 *Cultural Encounters in the U.S.A.*

Follow-ups

1A Howard mentions the dedicated nature of true fans on the West Coast, who will watch sports at ten o'clock in the morning. With time-zone differences in the United States, it is twelve noon in New York when it is six in the morning in Hawaii. People living in these various time zones are used to planning their TV-watching hours to accommodate the time differences. Choose another answer.

14B Right! This is an event only for women and girls. The tradition is for the bride to turn her back and toss her flowers to the unmarried females at the reception. The folk belief is that whoever catches the bouquet will be the next one to get married. Since the girl is only ten, she will not be getting married for a long time.

27C Local leash laws require that owners keep control of their pets. Unleashed pets must remain on their owners' premises. Compared to other parts of the world, there are few animals roaming freely in the cities of the United States. There is no reason to believe that Chief's leash is improper. Find a better answer.

40D Americans refer to some brown-skinned people as black, but only those whose racial ancestry is Negro. A brown-skinned-native Hawaiian, for example, would be considered Polynesian, not black. Look for a more specific explanation.

2A   He might want Wally to join him in an after-dinner game. Marsha says she wants him to share both the fun and the work of the household. In this scene, however, there is something else David expects of Wally before they relax.

15B   Many people start their day with a cup of coffee. The caffeine in coffee seems to help them wake up. Both these men say they enjoy drinking coffee, so it is unlikely that they would skip it this morning. John has something else in mind.

28C   At first, Tony said he wanted to stay home to watch the TV news and have some Chinese food delivered. After Rosa suggested going out, he said "I could get up for that," indicating that he was interested in her idea and would cheerfully go to Al's. Try again.

41D   Tara insists on paying her own way—"going dutch," she calls it. Unless two people are dating, it is common for each to pay his or her own way at social outings. It is unlikely that Tara allowed Ari to pay for her ticket without reimbursement.

3A *Fixed* can mean "prepared," so most meals are fixed, but in this sentence it means "set in time or manner," and this does not apply. There is no mention of time, but the phrase "Every man for himself" means that each person fixes his or her own breakfast. This implies that the Gransees eat whenever and whatever they want for that meal.

16B There is usually no relationship between arriving early and leaving early. Guests arrive early in order to mingle, or mix, with other guests. Dinner starts at eight and lasts usually until ten or ten-thirty.

29C Gambling, along with driving laws, the sale and distribution of alcohol, and the registration of guns, is regulated by individual states. While gambling is illegal in most states, it is legal in Nevada, where Anita will go to the Las Vegas casinos. Try another answer.

42D To see how much Becker earns, one must consult the scale of pay for GS (Government Service) employees. The lowest paid are GS-1s; the highest paid are GS-16s. These numbers, however, do not directly relate to any specific amount; salaries change as the cost of living changes. Why do you think Becker answered the way he did?

4A   Kirk indicated that he thought a dry white wine would be good with their food. This is the kind of wine many people drink with a light meal or with fish or fowl as the main dish. Anyone using Kirk's description would be able to choose an acceptable wine. This is not Kirk's concern.

17B   Fred was late for work and Erica commented on it in a friendly way. She then immediately introduced him to Abile, indicating that she was not very upset. Fred was not talking about lateness.

30C   Many Texans have one-syllable names. Those who live outside their state are sometimes called Tex. Using a shortened form of a person's name, however, is not limited to Texas. It is practiced throughout the country, and not "all" Texans have such names. Find a more specific answer.

43D   This is what Kwan is trying to do. He thinks he is complimenting his hosts for the fine food. He does not realize that burping is unacceptable table manners in the United States. In some countries, the cook would be surprised if you did not burp after a meal; in North America, however, the opposite is true.

5A   We do not know if this is his first visit to the United States. Estela has described many of the day's activities, so he knows what will happen. Paco will also see many signs of patriotism on this day. American flags will fly and the colors of the flag—red, white, and blue—will be everywhere.

18B Negotiating a price can be very tricky. The buyer has to decide how much the item is worth, and the seller has to make a profit. The problem Soong had at the department store, however, was not about the offer of a specific amount. Look further for the answer.

31C At first this casual remark seems appropriate for informal Americans. However, it does not show sympathy. In paying their respects, the students should offer encouragement and allow Nan to indicate how she is dealing with the death of her mother. Look for a better response.

44D Beach passes are sold by the day, the week, and the season in most beach towns. Guards patrol the beaches to check that all bathers have their passes. Victor's and Flor's passes may be good for one day, but they will not expire until the beach closes today. This is not why Flor wants to leave the beach.

6A   Sports are popular shows on American television. Several stations show only sports events. Many games are in the evening and on weekends. The most-watched events are the World Series (baseball), the Super Bowl (professional football), and the Kentucky Derby (horse racing). However, Mieko says she is not a sports fan, so they probably will not watch the baseball game. Try again.

19B   Customers are expected to tip the waiter or waitress, but not the busboy. Tip the bartender only when ordering directly at the bar. Try again.

32C   In many cultures, when a person admires something you own, you offer to give it to him or her. This is not widely practiced in the United States. Some people, especially teenagers, lend each other clothes. Juan should not feel any obligation to give James his jacket, but he might lend it to him on occasion. This is not what caused surprise in Juan.

45D   This is correct. The dress code is less formal in North America than Flor is used to. Her discomfort is based on a general feeling that she is not dressed formally enough. In warm weather, many Americans wear shorts and other such casual clothes in suburban neighborhoods outside of big cities.

7A   The clerk uses the term *all right*, which means "correct" or "okay." The clerk is telling Mbele that he will be at the place he wants to go. *Right* can also mean the opposite of *left*, indicating a side of the road. This clue might help you find the right answer.

20B Correct! Immigrants from many countries settled in Eastern and Midwestern industrial cities such as Milwaukee, Cleveland, Philadelphia, and Baltimore. While formally known as Polish-Americans and Italo-Americans, many refer to themselves simply as Polish or Italian. Theo is a second-generation Greek-American, who refers to himself as Greek.

33C Some teenagers attend parties on dates as couples; others go in groups. The practice differs depending on local custom. Linda does not ask Juan to go out with only her; she asks if he wants to "come along" with "a bunch of us." She would have used other words to indicate that she wanted to go together with him as a couple. Look again.

46D If no one in the office smokes, there would be no smokers, except Kokei, at the lunch table. This is, however, a matter of individual choice, not an extension of company rules outside the workplace. There is no reason to think that office rules extend beyond the office. Look for a more reasonable answer.

8A   This is the correct answer. A *homeroom* is a classroom where students of the same grade meet for announcements and to study. It is often the first class of the day. No subject matter is taught in a homeroom. Mary and Nguyen are on their way to report to their homeroom.

21B   They are assuming this because they heard Debbie repeat the surgeon's words: "I can't operate on this child—he's my son." This assumption, however, is not keeping them from solving the riddle; something else is.

34C   Alan says he has been trying to lose weight, but the suit was much too large to account for weight loss. What would explain the fact that his regular size (forty-eight) is so big on him?

47D   Friday afternoons, after work, are usually busy times for bars and restaurants. Many have happy hours with special prices and free food. The practice of offering free non-alcoholic drinks to designated drivers, however, is an individual bar's decision. It is not a law; it is simply this bar's practice.

9A   The job of a counterman is to take customers' orders and serve them. He didn't misunderstand; he just wanted to take Kim's order. This clue should help you choose the correct answer.

22B   Correct! *You all,* or *y'all,* is a common expression among Southerners. It means "you" in both singular and plural.

35C   Short delays of five to ten minutes usually require no apology. When the wait is fifteen minutes or longer, some apology and explanation of the lateness is normal and expected. This clue should help you determine what the dean was doing.

48D   Correct. A "right-to-work" state is one that has passed laws preventing unions from requiring membership as a prerequisite (something that is necessary) to employment. Most "right-to-work" states are in the Sunbelt and in the Midwest. Among union members, these are very controversial laws.

10A   Supermarket checkout lines are designed so that shoppers can place goods on the conveyer belt while they wait their turn. In an express line, several shoppers can place their groceries on the belt while they wait. Maria and Iris probably already had their items on the belt, so the checker meant something else.

23B   Benigno says, "People warned me it was cold . . . ." He probably knew about the snow, too, even if he had never seen any. This is not what he forgot.

36C   This is the most likely answer. Modern malls are clean, attractive, pleasant places. Many are physically agreeable, too—with air-conditioning, enclosed archways, and trees lining the pathways. Today's malls serve the same function as main shopping streets in villages. Going shopping can be a social event.

49D   Westerners are known to play jokes on people. Typically, residents of remote or isolated areas, such as the Rocky Mountain states, are friendly, easy-going, and playful. Misleading a tourist who is looking for somewhere to stay, however, is not typical Western humor. Grady was referring to something else.

11A His concern is that the teacher does not like him. In his culture, a student looking the teacher in the eye would be considered impolite. In this culture, he would be considered confident. Li is worried, but not about his schoolwork. Try another answer.

24B Some people believe that it is bad luck to talk about certain things before they happen. They think, for example, that if they talk about a job they are interested in before someone actually offers it to them, they will not be offered the job. There is no such folk belief, however, related to birthday parties. Janet has something else in mind.

37C Years ago, children would offer to do tricks in return for small treats. Later, the custom became that children would play a trick on anyone who did not offer them a treat; the tricks are usually harmless.

50D People tend to get separated in large crowds, so it is possible that Carla will have difficulty rounding up the other three people, but this is not indicated in the dialogue. She suggests taking two taxis for another reason.

12A   Correct! She believes that a girl should hug only the boy she is going out with, or dating. She believes that if she hugs a boy, he will think she is interested in an intimate relationship with him. In fact, in the United States, many people of both sexes hug each other to show affection and friendship.

25B   Some scientists typically wear white laboratory coats when they are working. When they are not working, however, their clothing choices are individual.

38C   Correct! This is accepted behavior in many countries. It is much less trouble to settle an infraction immediately and not have to go through the red tape, or unnecessary rules, to settle it later. Rodolfo says he wants to "settle this . . . now." The traffic officer however, tells Rodolfo to put his money away, indicating that she will not accept it. It is also possible that the traffic officer thought Rodolfo was trying to bribe her; bribery, or trying to influence an official unfairly, is illegal in the United States.

51D   This is possible, but not probable. In any event, if he were jealous, he would show it in a different way. The phrase Colson uses has a specific meaning to performers.

13A Mac was being kind to Steve. People often support friends by encouraging them and, occasionally, pretending not to notice poor performances. When Jorge commented on Steve's playing, he was telling the truth. Steve probably was not insulted by this. He changed the subject for another reason. Find a better answer.

26B Parents often give out the presents that are under the tree on Christmas morning so that each child has something to open. In many families, people exchange gifts before breakfast while still in their pajamas. It is unlikely that many fathers dress up in red suits. Try another answer.

39C This is one of the two correct answers explaining the confusion. In many parts of the world, the first floor is the one above the ground level. In the United States, the first floor is the ground level, so the second floor in Philadelphia would be the same as the first floor in the Soviet Union. Look for the other explanation, since this accounts for only one floor; Alexi's count was off by two.

52D No doubt the confusion and mess have made May a little nervous. She wants to organize the office and does not want anything to go wrong; this is why she refers to several different irrational folk beliefs. This clue should help lead you to the correct answer.

14A It is true that weddings can be expensive. Traditionally, the bride's parents provide the food and drinks for all the guests and pay for all related expenses. In some cases, the couple shares the expense. The cost, however, is not what Sam is talking about.

27B Correct! Most restaurants in the United States do not allow animals. This restriction is enforced by local laws and regulations, normally for reasons of health and sanitation. Exceptions are made for dogs that help blind people. From the dialogue, we have no evidence that Chief has been trained for this purpose.

40C This is the correct answer. African-Americans have been called Negro, colored, and black. Because of its easy contrast with *white*, or Caucasian, *black* is still used primarily to describe race or skin color even for African-Americans who are light brown.

1D This may or may not be true, depending on local customs. It is very common for American football fans to have drinks and light foods while watching sporting events. The most common snacks served are potato chips, pretzels, peanuts, and other foods that can be eaten with the fingers.

15A   Some restaurants open as early as five o'clock in the morning, but not many. It is possible that John knows of one and wants to stop and eat, but it is not likely. He wants to get out on the water before the sun rises. He has something else in mind.

28B   Diners who go to all-you-can-eat restaurants sometimes order only the salad bar. They fill their plates with fruits, vegetables, bread, and sauces. Rosa might want to do this, but Tony is suggesting something else. What is it?

41C   Ari mentions that he read a review of the movie, and Tara indicates that she knows it is a light comedy. These clues tell you that they both have an idea of what they are going to see. Films are reviewed in newspapers and on television when they are first released in the theaters. People talk about movies they have seen, too. As a result, most moviegoers know something about the movie before going to see it. Try again.

2D   This is what David expects. The Gransees explain that everyone in the family shares not only in the fun but also in the work. Guests in an informal home atmosphere such as this one help either prepare the meal or clean up after it.

16A   Chan is wary of arriving early because of her previous experience at the cookout. She does not want to be the first to arrive. Her friend would understand this concern. Try another answer.

29B   Scientists often keep their work secret until reporting on it in professional journals, or magazines. Research labs often have strict security and secrecy requirements for their employees. Anita, however, was talking about her vacation plans, which have nothing to do with her work. Look for another answer.

42C   Some people are lazy; this is true in all professions. Lazy people generally do not receive promotions and therefore do not earn as much as harder-working employees. There may be some exceptions to this, but not many. Find a better answer.

3D   Marsha assures Wally that he will never go to bed hungry, meaning he will always be well fed. The general tone of the conversation indicates that quantity or presence of food is not a problem in this house. The Gransees probably go to the supermarket at least once a week. Try again.

17A   Correct! Several standard informal greetings are used in the dialogue (*How's it going?*, *How are you doing?*, and *What's happening?*). These expressions are heard among friends and acquaintances. They require no specific response, because they mean the same as *Hello*.

30B   We rarely refer to or address a person by his or her complete name. Usually we use the first name or a title and the last (family) name. For example, Robert Garcia might be addressed as Bob or Mr. Garcia but not as Robert Garcia. This, however, is not why the oil drillers shortened Lamchul's name. Find a better reason.

43C   Stomach gas builds up from various foods we eat, and we expel it. In the United States, this response is considered inappropriate, so most people cover their mouths and burp silently. But everyone belches, including Alaskans. Try again.

4D   This is the most probable answer. It is against the law for Claude to buy the wine. He is twelve years old, a minor. In most states, a minor is anyone under twenty-one, although it can be as low as eighteen. Minors may not buy alcoholic beverages. If a person trying to buy beer, wine, or liquor looks younger than twenty-one, he or she may be asked to produce proof of age.

18A	It is always a good idea to study people and their customs when living in a foreign country. Soong already has some negotiating skills, and he might learn other techniques from David. This, however, is not the problem he had at the department store.

31B	Many cultures react to death with great public grief and expressions of despair. Americans tend to offer encouragement to close friends and relatives of a dead person. This expression would be received as overly gloomy. Try another one.

44C	Boardwalks have many stands selling fried foods and sweet treats. There are also souvenir stores that sell small gifts and beach supplies, as well as amusement park games and rides. Victor seems interested in doing some shopping, but we have no evidence that Flor is. Look for a more likely answer.

5D	The activities mentioned—sports, barbecuing food, speeches—all usually involve crowds. Since he is looking forward to the day, we can assume that large groups of people will not be a problem for him. His remark about noise is the key to understanding what he expects in the evening.

19A   Most restaurants add a gratuity, or tip, only for large groups eating together. Adding fifteen percent is not commonly practiced in North America. When this is done, it is clearly marked on the bill.

32B   Americans often give compliments freely, that is, with no expectations other than to make a person feel comfortable. Juan may or may not be used to compliments, but this is not what he is reacting to.

45C   Flor does not know the dress code for amusement parks, so she asks her friend. Trish assures her that her clothes are appropriate. A day at a park means a lot of walking under the hot sun. People dress as comfortably as possible, with many wearing shorts. Flor's discomfort goes beyond her concern over the cleanliness of her shorts.

6D   Since these are the only shows on, besides the baseball game, which Mieko does not want to watch, this is probably what they will watch. The "season" for first-run shows and movies is from the fall through the spring. Advertisers are usually unwilling to pay for new shows during the summer, when fewer people watch TV.

20A Since he thinks Theo's references are to foreigners, he is surprised; but he is not worried. He does not know how Theo is using these ethnic references. This clue should help you choose the correct answer.

33B Correct! This is the most likely conclusion from the dialogue clues. Linda says "a bunch of us kids" will meet and walk together. High schoolers commonly go in groups to concerts, parties, and sporting events. Teenagers are often more comfortable with boy-girl relationships in a crowd, rather than one-on-one.

46C This is the most likely answer. The average restaurant today has a nonsmoking section, and nonsmokers normally choose to sit in it. If Kokei wants to smoke, he will have to do it before entering the restaurant.

7D In the United States, as in the rest of the world, only about ten percent of people are born naturally left-handed. Usually, a person's ability to drive a car or learn local traffic patterns is not affected by right-handedness or left-handedness.

21A   At first Maria assumed that the father wasn't badly hurt; then Debbie verified that he had serious injuries. So Maria could no longer assume this. Try again.

34B   Right you are! Alan's size forty-eight suit in Peru is a size thirty-eight here. His thirty-nine shirt is called a fifteen and a half here. Men's dress shirts are sized according to collar and sleeve length. Exact measurements are important. More casual shirts are sized as small (S), medium (M), large (L), and extra large (XL). Pants are measured by inches, too, for waist size and length. It is a good idea for travelers to carry a conversion chart to help with different measurement systems.

47C   Alcoholic drinks usually cost more than nonalcoholic ones. Occasionally, a bar offers something on its menu for free, usually as an encouragement for customers to buy other items. It is not a common practice, however, to charge only for alcoholic beverages.

8D   Teenagers often use a kind of insulting humor, especially with their best friends. Mary and Chuck enjoy teasing each other, but Mary's suggestion that they hurry to their homeroom is not a joke.

22A The passenger was being friendly and engaging in small talk, or unimportant conversation. She did not want him to travel with her; she was simply asking about his travel plans. Find another answer.

35B Isabel was late yesterday, and she missed her appointment. Today she arrived on time. We know from the dialogue that they have been in the office for fifteen minutes. They were due at three-fifteen and it is now three-thirty. They were not late. Who was?

48C At one time, almost all auto manufacturing jobs were centered around the Great Lakes states. Nowadays, however, auto parts are manufactured in virtually every state. It is not true that auto-related jobs are not available in the North.

9D A delicatessen sells sandwiches, salads, and other prepared foods. This one offers sandwiches made of cold cuts (and probably many other items as well). The counterman is asking Kim for his order, which he calls a *hero*. This clue should give you the right answer.

23A It is certainly true that keeping warm is necessary when visiting a place where the snows can last five days to six months. He may have forgotten his warm clothes when leaving the Philippines, but we cannot know this from the dialogue. It was something else he forgot.

36B By using the pronoun *we*, Grace indirectly offers to accompany Ana when she returns Alan's shirt. Grace is happy to go along with her friend, and there is no reason to think she is making the offer simply to be polite. Modern shopping malls are safe, pleasant environments. Friends with free time often spend time together in places like shopping malls. Does this clue help you find the right answer?

49C This is the correct answer. Wyoming's towns are few and far apart. People who live there tend to minimize the distances between them and the time it takes to travel to them. What is considered "down the road a piece," a short distance to a Westerner, may be a great distance to anyone else.

10D Modern supermarkets sell many nonfood products such as soap, kitchen utensils, and personal-hygiene items. Checkers at all lines are able to scan and charge for anything bought in the store. Look for another explanation.

24A   Janet is reasonably certain that it will not rain on Saturday, because, in Hawaii, it rains only during certain seasons or times of day. We can infer from the conversation that this is not one of those. She says, "Here we know when it's going to rain," and no one would plan a beach party if it were going to rain. Find another answer.

37B   This is the best answer. The phrase *trick or treat* literally asks the question, "Would you like me to play a trick on you, or will you give me a treat?" In modern practice, however, it means "May I show you my costume, and will you put a treat in my bag?" It is a standard saying, used only on this occasion. Children out in costumes on October 31 are often called trick-or-treaters.

50C   This is the most likely answer. Sense of personal space is a highly individual feeling, but generally, North Americans tend to need more of it than Latin Americans or Asians. Raul did not mind the thought of six people (including the driver) riding together. Carla already indicated that she did not like the crowded feeling at the exhibit. She will probably insist that the five of them go in two separate cars.

11D   Correct! In North America, people expect to look into the eyes of the person they are speaking to. Looking down or looking away is a sign of uncertainty and lack of self-confidence. Students are expected to volunteer the answer to a question in a forthright, or direct, manner. Speaking up confidently is considered an admirable quality.

25A *Casual* means "informal" to everyone. Some groups, by individual choice, define informality by wearing blue jeans and running shoes. There is nothing specific about journalists that defines what they wear to a party.

38B Sometimes police officers let offenders go with just a warning (and a lecture). There is no indication here that Rodolfo will receive such a warning. He will probably get the ticket as it was written. Look for another solution.

51C Branca's reference to "tripping over his lines" means he hopes he does not make a mistake in the words to his songs. A verbal stumble is certainly different from a physical one, and Colson knows this difference. This is not what he meant.

12D Most people are wary of activities and behavior they do not understand. Elsa, however, thinks she does understand the custom of hugging, and she does not approve of it. What she does not understand is that, in North America, hugging means something different from what it means where she comes from.

26A   A traditional Christmas dinner includes a turkey that is carved and served at the table. Other traditional foods are cranberries, green beans, and mashed potatoes. Often family members visit on this holiday, and many Christmas dinners are large. The reference to the red-suited man, however, has nothing to do with the dinner. Try another answer.

39B   This is one of the two correct answers explaining the confusion. For many reasons, the number thirteen is considered unlucky in North America. Many people would refuse to sleep in a hotel room on the thirteenth floor. To avoid problems, hotels number their stories eleven, twelve, fourteen, fifteen, etc. Look for the other explanation, since this accounts for only one floor; Alexi's count was off by two.

52C   Right you are! The old folk belief is that breaking a mirror will bring seven years of bad luck. The origins of such superstitions are mostly unknown. Few people actually believe them, but many act as if they do.

13D   Many men in the United States have difficulties discussing their feelings. They seem more comfortable talking about impersonal aspects of life rather than personal ones. This is not true of all men, however, so it cannot be said that "men never discuss their feelings." Try another answer.

27A Diners often have "short order" menus, which means food that is prepared and served quickly. It would be common to find frankfurters on this kind of menu. Some dogs eat this kind of food. This is not why Pam wants to take Chief home. Look further.

40B Americans use the word *brown* to describe a person's skin color, but not as frequently as in other cultures. In much of Latin America, for example, using the word for brown to describe someone is a compliment. Find a more likely answer.

1C Jorge mentions that he knows the games are different, even though the word *football* in Spanish refers to a different sport. The most popular sport in the world is known as soccer in the United States. Try again.

14D Many of the traditions surrounding a marriage ceremony have to do with wishing good luck. Tossing rice (or bird seed) gently over the couple's heads as they leave the ceremony is a symbol of good luck. It is considered bad luck for the groom to see the bride right before the ceremony, but throwing the bouquet is not associated with luck. Try again.

28A Diners who wish to take home any uneaten food from their plates often request that the waiter or waitress put it in a bag called a doggie bag. Most restaurants provide this service. It is a joke that the food will be taken to the dog, since many people do not have a dog. Find another answer.

41B Right you are! Concession stands or snack bars (usually in the lobby of the theater) are popular in the United States. Many people, like Tara, buy popcorn, candy, and soda to take to their seats, eating and drinking silently during the movie. She wishes they had remembered to stop at the stand before going to their seats.

2C He probably does want Wally to call him by his first name. In a family setting such as this, everyone uses each other's first name. What David expects, however, has to do with his action of standing after the meal. Does this clue help?

15D Some people enjoy coffee only when it is brewed, that is, when the ground coffee beans are combined with hot water and then strained. Others drink instant coffee. It is both a matter of personal taste and of available time; brewing coffee takes longer. We have no evidence how John likes his coffee. Try again.

29A Singh has been on the job for only three days, so he might be worried about Anita's leaving. She, on the other hand, seems to have confidence in his ability; she tells him that he is a good scientist. She has also acquainted him with the project and the laboratory. Try another one.

42B Good answer! A GS (for Government Service) number indicates rank and pay. Becker is high on the scale and probably receives an excellent salary. Anyone who knows the scale, which is public knowledge, will know how much Becker earns. It is considered impolite, however, to ask someone his or her earnings, so Becker deals with the question by answering indirectly.

3C There is no mention of regularity in the dialogue; however, most American homes have regular mealtimes because people work regular hours. The Gransees probably eat dinner within two hours of returning from work.

16D Correct! At formal, sit-down dinner parties, guests are expected to arrive some time before dinner is served. They mingle with other guests, eat hors d'oeuvres, and perhaps have a cocktail until being seated for dinner. It is considered impolite to arrive after guests have been seated and dinner has begun.

30A   Correct! People often show newcomers that they are welcome by addressing them informally, without titles (Mr., Ms., Dr., etc.). In this case, they shortened his name, much the same way Beauregard was shortened to Bo. The country bar atmosphere is friendly and informal. Bo, Red, and Sis want to show Adiprachan that he is among friends.

43B   Traditionally, the father of the family sits at the head of the table and carves the meat. He may even start the passing of the other dishes, although at this meal he asks his wife to start passing the potatoes. There is no tradition, however, for burping at the table, because it is considered impolite.

4C   Many cooks want some time alone in the kitchen when they are preparing meals, but there is no indication of this from Kirk. He wants Jean to accompany his nephew for another reason.

17D   Abile responded to the person who spoke directly to him. In short social situations, speaking to one person at a time is considered polite, not a mistake.

31A This is the best answer. The thought conveyed by this expression of sympathy is direct. It shows concern for Nan. Her students probably did not know Nan's mother, so they could not say anything about the woman.

44B This is the most likely answer. The late-summer sun along the East Coast of the United States can be strong enough to burn one's skin. People who are not used to the sun stay only a short time; then they cover their skin or get out of the sun's direct rays. Flor wants to be careful since they have been on the beach "a few hours."

5C The picnicking part of the Fourth of July celebration usually happens during the day. Paco's final remark about noise is not about food. This clue should help.

18D There are several terms used to describe sales of used or contributed items; some common names are *rummage sales, yard sales, garage sales, tag sales,* and *flea markets.* Bargain hunters shop at these, but not exclusively. They also shop at stores, particularly during special sales. Try not to confuse the noun *bargain* (something bought cheaply) with the verb (to negotiate the price and conditions of a sale).

32A Bill and Diane both praise his language ability. In order to be courteous, many people commend, or speak favorably of, a person's abilities. They probably sincerely appreciate his proficiency and accent. His surprise, however, has nothing to do with this. Look further.

45B Flor wonders if she is dressed appropriately for a restaurant, and Trish assures her that she is. Amusement parks and their restaurants have a casual dress code. Flor's discomfort is deeper than her concern over how she will look in a restaurant.

6C It's true that they are tired, but Mieko says she wants to "turn it on anyway," in the hopes that some show will be interesting. In some homes, people leave the TV on almost as a background for whatever else is going on. They occasionally look over at the set to see if something interesting is on.

19D The standard policy in North America is for customers to tip the waiter or waitess fifteen to twenty percent of the restaurant bill, depending on the quality of the service. Waiters and waitresses earn most of their income through tips, not salary. Knowing this should lead you to the correct answer.

33A Generally, boys ask girls for dates, but not always. In many communities, it is equally appropriate for both boys and girls to ask each other out on dates. Linda did not ask Juan on a date this time, but she might in the future. Try again.

46B Some local laws ban smoking from all public places, including shopping malls and restaurants. The number of cities and towns with such policies is growing. Across the United States, however, not many restaurants are completely smoke-free. This is not a law on Long Island.

7C Correct! In Kenya, Mbele drives on the left-hand side. Now he must change his driving habits and learn to drive on the right-hand side. A left-hand turn lane helps drivers (who are driving on the right-hand side of the road) cross over against oncoming traffic.

20D He may have been aware of the widespread cultural and ethnic diversity; many people know about the "melting pot." But we cannot know one way or another from the dialogue. His confusion lies elsewhere. Choose another answer.

34A   Some men's clothing stores are specialty shops that carry only large sizes. A large department store, however, would stock suits and shirts for the average-sized man. There is no reason to think this is a specialty shop.

47B   Bars offer discount drinks during "happy hour," which is usually between five and seven o'clock. The idea is to attract people to come after work, before they go home. Some offer drinks at reduced prices; others give free food. There is no policy, however, of offering free drinks based on nationality.

8C   Some schools have registration on the same day that classes start, but most have it a day or two before the academic year begins. We know from the dialogue that registration was yesterday and that Mary and Nguyen are now on their way to their homeroom.

21D   Correct! In fact, the child's mother was the surgeon. But Mario and Maria both automatically assumed, as do many people, that a surgeon must be a man. In the United States, fifteen percent of doctors are women, and thirty-one percent of current medical-school students are female.

35A Busy people in all professions occasionally fall behind in keeping to their schedules. University deans are no exception, but they are not known for keeping people waiting. Professional people generally consider punctuality important, so they keep appointments at the agreed time. Find another answer.

48B The so-called Rust Belt states of the North have, indeed, been declining in population and jobs in recent years. The sunnier states of the Sunbelt are attracting industry, and workers are following the employment opportunities. These trends vary from year to year and from industry to industry, so this generalization cannot be proved. Look for a more specific reason.

9C   There are many kinds of hoagies (and submarine sandwiches and heroes). This is a type of sandwich that has many ingredients on a small loaf of bread. Delicatessens that sell these kinds of sandwiches often advertise that fact in their signs outside. This clue should lead you to the right answer.

22D Train travel in the United States is generally comfortable and efficient. The schedules are easy to read, and the railroad workers are usually courteous. Mahmoud knew he was on the right train because he asked the conductor. Look for another answer.

36A   Of course shopping centers exist as market places. Shoppers spend money at the stores, restaurants, and service establishments—it is the capitalist system. This time, however, Grace probably wants to go there for another reason. Try again.

49B   The distance between towns can be a hundred miles (160 kilometers) or more. The entire state of Wyoming has fewer people than the city of San Francisco. This would account for difficulty in finding a town, but it does not explain what Grady said. He was responding to the answer given by the auto mechanic.

10C   All checkout aisles usually display the same tabloids. The headlines are often strange and hard to believe but are always eye-catching. The checker was noting something about the women's purchases, not about tabloids. Try another answer.

23D   Americans who live in northern and western mountain areas are more accustomed to winter than those who live in the warmer South and Southwest, where it rarely goes below freezing. So only some of the people are used to cold weather.

37A On Halloween, many children dress up as superheroes such as Batman or Superman or as supernatural creatures such as monsters and ghosts. The children dressed as ghosts are only pretending to be scary creatures. They jokingly "scare" adults for another purpose. What is it?

50B Taxis in Chicago are the same as taxis elsewhere in the United States. They come in all shapes and sizes, all makes and models of cars. Most are full-sized, seating five or six people comfortably.

11C Li probably is a little afraid of, or intimidated by, the teacher. She wants him to look her in the eye and speak out. This is a behavior he is not used to; he thinks it is impolite. This is a concern for him, but another answer is more complete. Try again.

24D Correct! The idea is for Jose to take Andy out in the ocean in order to get him away from the beach while his friends set up a party. They hope to surprise him when he comes out of the water. Surprise birthday parties are a tradition in many parts of the U.S.

38A As in other countries, people who break traffic laws often plead ignorance, hoping to avoid paying fines. Depending on the circumstances, they might even be successful. It is possible that Rodolfo wanted to do this, but it is not likely since: (a) the traffic officer had already written the ticket, and (b) he was taking money out of his wallet.

51B Correct. No one knows for certain where this particular phrase originated, or why it means "good luck." The phrase is now used in common speech when someone is embarking on a new venture, or beginning a new project.

12C She may be jealous of Dana's popularity, but her objections are based on Dana's behavior. There is no concrete evidence that this is the correct answer. Try again.

25D This is the most likely answer. Gina probably thought about the general dress code of professionals, realized what people at a conference would wear, and advised Doris to wear what she wore the previous night. There is no easy answer to this question of "casual" dress. You have to know more about the situation and the people. It is always best to ask.

39A Alexi does seem to be stubborn because he keeps insisting he is right. Strongly held beliefs, however, can be proven correct by checking the facts; the fact is that he was able to count only twelve stories. The explanation lies in two other answers.

52B According to an old folk belief, walking under a ladder is supposed to bring bad luck. It is similar to another, which predicts terrible things will happen if a black cat crosses one's path. Few people actually believe these superstitions, but many refer to them. May's reference is to another superstitious belief.

13C Right you are. Problems between husbands and wives is a very personal subject. Most people feel comfortable discussing such matters only with close friends. By changing the topic, Steve was politely saying that the subject was too sensitive or personal to discuss with Jorge.

26D Christmas Day, December 25, is usually cold in the Midwest, and it often snows. Traditionally, snow is part of the festive holiday atmosphere in this part of the country. While some snowstorms are loud, this is not what Mr. Helms is talking about. Look for a reference to another tradition.

40A Cinnamon is usually dark brown with some light brown highlights. It is not a word used frequently to describe skin color, even though it is descriptive of many people's coloring. Melina's answer had nothing to do with cinnamon. Try another answer.

1B Correct! The words *cowboys* and *redskins* are also used in movies about the Old West. Teams in the National Football League have many colorful nicknames. Some are animals: Chicago Bears, Indianapolis Colts, Los Angeles Rams; some are birds: Philadelphia Eagles, Atlanta Falcons, Phoenix Cardinals; and some are a mix of unusual words: New York Jets, Pittsburgh Steelers, San Francisco 49ers, New Orleans Saints. The Dallas team is called the Cowboys, while the Washington team is called the Redskins.

14C Some people feel strongly about tradition; they don't like to change custom. It could be that Sam disapproves of the couple's using their own words for the ceremony, but we have no evidence. Look further.

27D Many people are afraid of dogs that are not under their owners' control. Fear of animals is one reason that leash laws are so widespread. However, this is not the reason Pam wants to take Chief home. Find a more specific reason.

41A In some countries, it is customary to tip the usher who shows you to your seat. In most American movie theaters, there are no ushers showing people to their seats. When there are ushers, it is not customary to tip them.

2B Sometimes houseguests prepare their own specialties. Wally may choose to cook the Gransees a Polish meal some evening. He would not, however, be expected to learn Marsha's grandmother's recipe for this traditional beef dinner.

15C This is the most likely answer. Many convenience stores are open twenty-four hours a day. John says he has been going fishing this early for years, so he probably knows of a store that is open at five o'clock. They will be able to get coffee and any other food they want to take with them. Most customers spend fewer than three minutes in a convenience store.

28D Correct! Rosa expressed concern at leaving uneaten food behind. Tony assured her that they could take it with them in a bag known as a doggie bag. Most restaurants provide this service. The joke is that the food in the bag will go to the diner's dog, while it is usually eaten by humans at a later time at home.

42A   Becker indicates that government salaries are comparable to those outside federal service. Much of the economy of Washington, D.C., is dependent on the federal government and its enormous payroll. The average employee earns enough to enjoy a reasonably good, middle-class life. Did Becker answer the question?

3B   Correct! The descriptions of different types of dinners, sending out for pizza, and going to a restaurant all indicate that there is variety in both what is eaten and where it is eaten.

16C   It is true that when a sit-down dinner party begins at eight, guests often arrive for hors d'oeuvres and cocktails around seven o'clock. This is not a fixed schedule, however. They would not be late unless they arrived after eight o'clock. Try again.

29D   Correct! Many people consider gambling as a vice, or an example of evil living. Anita does not want her boss to know that she likes to gamble for fear he will disapprove. She assumed it was okay to tell Singh, her coworker, but it was too risky to tell her boss. She did not lie directly, but she hid the complete truth.

43A Rachel is surprised that Kwan made this noise, and she might be embarrassed in front of her other guests. Belching in public is considered impolite in the United States. She may laugh gently at his social error in table manners, but she is probably not angry.

4B It is true that the boy has probably never been in that neighborhood before. People of all ages can lose their way; therefore, this is a possibility. Kirk's concern, however, is specifically about buying the wine. Does this clue help?

17C Abile was correct in responding to Fred, but the response was wrong. Fred was only saying hello. Abile could have shaken Fred's hand, but it would have been inappropriate to ask him the same question. Try another answer.

30D It is true that many Thai names seem long and difficult to pronounce. Many have five or six syllables, whereas the average American name has three or fewer. It is also true that Americans come from all the world's cultures; therefore, many have names that are long and multisyllabic. This answer is not complete enough.

44A Victor might enjoy watching women walk along the shore, and Flor might become jealous, but we do not know this from the dialogue. Her suggestion is based on something else.

5B This is the most likely answer. Paco's reference to noise is about the practice of setting off firecrackers at night. Most Fourth of July celebrations end in the evening, just after dark, with a display of loud, colorful fireworks.

18C Right you are! Most stores, especially large ones, have fixed prices, so buyers cannot negotiate with salesclerks. You will not have much success bargaining at a department store, for example. Rummage sales, yard sales, and garage sales are good places to bargain.

31D Nan says she is glad her mother no longer has any pain. She is relieved that her mother no longer suffers from her illness. She is not, however, happy. She does not feel joy at the death, although she does feel a small comfort that her mother is out of pain. Try again.

45A Flor says she is tired after spending half the day at the beach. This might be a problem, but Flor's other statements indicate a deeper concern. Look for a more complete answer.

6B Late news shows are usually produced locally, that is, by the station showing the news. The network news shows are on around the dinner hour, six or seven o'clock. Nobuo reports that both the late news and the talk shows begin after ten-thirty, the time when Mieko says she will be asleep. They probably will not watch either of these shows.

19C This is correct. The tip may be paid in cash or charged to a credit card; many hotel restaurants also allow customers to charge both the meal and the tip to their room. The tip is not commonly added to the bill as it is in many other countries. When it is added, a restaurant employee will mark it on the bill.

32D Correct! Americans occasionally exaggerate a compliment to make it sound more sincere. Bill spoke of "fantastic grades," Diane said his accent was "perfect," and James said his jacket was the "nicest." These superlatives should be understood figuratively, not as literal, or exact, truths.

46A   Nonsmokers, particularly those who have recently quit, often object to others smoking in their presence. The office employees may or may not want Kokei to smoke at lunch, but this is not why Koichi said what he did. Look for a more specific answer.

7B   It is probably true that he has never driven before in the United States, but that is not why he is mixed up. The confusion is based on the right side/left side problem. In Kenya, Great Britain, and other countries where traffic drives on the left side of the road, even the steering wheels are reversed. They are on the right-hand side of the car. In the United States, steering wheels are on the left-hand side of the car. This clue will probably help you find the right answer.

20C   Many ethnic groups have facial or body characteristics that make them identifiable. Many Swedish-Americans, for example, have blond hair and fair skin. Theo may or may not look Greek, but this is not what is confusing to Rajib. Try again.

33D   The word *date* can mean any appointment or engagement. We can say, "I have a date (with the dentist) to have my teeth cleaned." In the context of boy-girl relationships, however, a date is for two people who are interested in each other romantically. Look for a better answer.

47A This is correct. Bars, of course, encourage people to drink, but they are also interested in keeping customers alive for future business. Many bars encourage the practice of having a designated driver by offering free service to this volunteer driver.

8B Most high schools finish classes in the afternoon around three o'clock. That is when these freshmen will be able to go home. Home is where people live, but a homeroom is something else. Registration is over and classes are beginning. Try again.

21C Many riddles often seem unsolvable. When a person cannot figure out a mystery, it appears there could be no answer. But riddles always have answers. It is unlikely they believed this one had no answer. Which answer is plausible?

34D It is true that, on the average, Latin American men tend to be smaller than their counterparts in the United States. These are statistical averages, however. This store no doubt carries Alan's size. What is the problem?

48A Haiti is a tropical country, and Haitians are therefore unaccustomed to living in areas where it snows and the temperature goes below freezing every winter. On the other hand, many Haitians have moved to southern Ontario, where winters are severe. This is not the reason Henri is moving to the Sunbelt.

9B Correct! Different parts of the country call the sandwiches described in the dialogue by different names. Three of these names are mentioned: hoagie, submarine sandwich (or sub), and hero.

22C As in most cultures, Americans often use colorful idioms in their informal conversation. He did not respond to the idiom "my neck of the woods," so he probably understood it. Instead, he responded to her use of another expression. Does this clue help you find the right answer?

35D Right you are! Fifteen minutes is not considered serious lateness, but it is enough of a delay to make necessary a small apology plus an explanation. Delays of forty-five minutes or more are considered major.

49A Grady is eager to see Yellowstone, which is over 400 miles (640 kilometers) from Cheyenne. He may want to drive as far as possible before stopping for the night, but there is no indication from the dialogue that this is true. Look for a more specific explanation.

10B This is correct. Many supermarkets have a line for ten or fifteen (or fewer) items, called the express line. Some of these accept cash only, while the regular lines usually also allow payment by check or credit card. Express lines are good for shoppers who are buying only a few things. Since the women had twenty items, they should have gone to one of the regular, non-express lines.

23C Correct! Harry meant thirty-five degrees Fahrenheit (which is two degrees Centigrade), whereas Benigno was thinking thirty-five degrees Centigrade (which is ninety-five degrees Fahrenheit). It is a good idea to keep a temperature chart with you until you get used to the different measuring system.

36D Teenagers frequently use the shopping mall as a social meeting place to be with their friends. Grace does not show that she is at all worried about her kids when she says they are at the mall, so there is no evidence that she wants to check up on them. This is not why she wants to go to the mall with Ana.

50A Raul says he likes the Puerto Rican's work, and perhaps he will buy some of it. Art being shown at a museum, however, would not be sold on the spot. Raul will have to contact the artist, or her agent, at a later time.

11B Jack says that he usually knows the correct answer. Li's problem is that he is reluctant to give the answer because he is afraid that he will be considered too forward, or too sure of himself. In his culture, assertiveness in young people is often discouraged. See if this clue helps you choose the correct answer.

24C She intends to set up a birthday party on the beach while Andy and Jose are scuba diving. She tells Jose to come out around two o'clock because that is when she plans for the party to begin. Look for another answer.

37D Children usually comment on each other's costumes, usually to praise them. Parents who make their children's costumes are especially interested in the comments of other parents. The phrase *trick or treat*, however, has nothing to do with costumes. Try again.

51A The fears Branca is experiencing are universal and understandable. The distances he will cover are great, and the audiences will be demanding. If a joke would help, no doubt Colson would tell one. The phrase he used, however, has another meaning, one that is meaningful to performers.

12B She believes that couples who are going out may hug each other, but not other people. This means that she disapproves of most people hugging each other, but this is not the same as "never." Look for a more exact answer.

25C *Casual* certainly indicates different dress codes to different people. It is best to know what people mean by words like *casual.* This answer, however, is too general. Find a more specific reason.

38D Having a ticket "fixed" means having it unofficially disregarded or excused. This is not common practice in the United States; however, people can contest, or argue about, any traffic or parking ticket by requesting a court hearing with a judge. Try another answer.

52A May's reference to Friday the 13th is based on an old superstition that any time the thirteenth of the month falls on a Friday, one should be careful.

13B Mac thinks that Steve is worried about marital difficulties, which affected his ability to play. Steve might like baseball better than racquetball, but we cannot know from the dialogue. His refusal to give a direct answer is due to something else. Try again.

26C Correct! The story is that Santa Claus lands his sleigh on the roof, climbs down the chimney, and distributes presents to all children. This jolly, overweight man with a white beard is seen wearing a red suit. It is believed that the many bells on his sleigh jingle when it flies, explaining Mr. Helms's reference to noise.

39D Philadelphia is not on a mountain. It is a fairly flat city, with two rivers running through it: the Delaware and the Schuylkill. There are two correct explanations for this confusion.

Topical Index

Topical Index

Animals	Walking the Dog	27
Clothing	What to Wear	25
	Dressed for the Occasion	45
Compliments	Really?	32
Daily Life	Everyday Meals	3
Death	A Death in the Family	31
Directions	On the Highway	49
Drinking	Designated Driver	47
Driving	The Right Way to Drive	7
	Designated Driver	47
	On the Highway	49
Ethnicity	Proud of Their Heritage	20
	Many Colors	40
Family	A Riddle	21
	A Death in the Family	31
Formality	Dinner at Eight	16
	Just Call Me Erica	17
	What to Wear	25
	Nicknames	30
	Dressed for the Occasion	45
Guest Behavior	One of the Family	2
	Dinner at Eight	16
	Table Manners	43
Greetings	Just Call Me Erica	17
Idiomatic Language	Traveling by Train	22
	Stage Fright	51
Jobs	The Right to Work	48
Laws	Wine with Dinner	4
	The Right Way to Drive	7
	Getting a Ticket	38
Meals	One of the Family	2
	Everyday Meals	3
	Wine with Dinner	4
	Sandwiches to Go	9
	Dinner at Eight	16

Meals *(Continued)*	How Much Should I Leave?	19
	Walking the Dog	27
	All You Can Eat	28
	Table Manners	43
	No Smoking	46
Money	Going Dutch	41
	How Much Do You Make?	42
Names	Just Call Me Erica	17
	Nicknames	30
Punctuality	Sorry I'm Late	35
Seasons	A Birthday on the Beach	24
School	Starting High School	8
	Participating in Class	11
Shopping	Bargain Hunting	18
Smoking	No Smoking	46
Social Interaction	Participating in Class	11
	An Innocent Hug	12
	Private Thoughts	13
	I Need This Vacation	29
	Really?	32
	Is It a Date?	33
	Sorry I'm Late	35
	At the Mall	36
	Going Dutch	41
	How Much Do You Make?	42
	Dressed For the Occasion	45
	A Bit Crowded	50
Special Days	Independence Day	5
	A Birthday on the Beach	24
	A Traditional Christmas	26
	Trick or Treat	37
Sports	Sunday Football	1
	Private Thoughts	13
Stereotypes	A Riddle	21
Stores	Sandwiches to Go	9

Stores *(Continued)*	At the Checkout Counter	10
	Strong Coffee	15
	Bargain Hunting	18
	The Right Size	34
	At the Mall	36
Superstition	The Missing Floor	39
	Seven Years of Bad Luck	52
Television	Sunday Football	1
	What's On?	6
Tipping	How Much Should I Leave?	19
Traditions	Here Comes the Bride	14
	A Traditional Christmas	26
	Trick or Treat	37
	The Missing Floor	39
	Seven Years of Bad Luck	52
Traveling	Traveling by Train	22
Vacations	I Need a Vacation	29
	Summer Sun	44
Weather	How Cold Is It?	23
	A Birthday on the Beach	24
Weddings	Here Comes the Bride	14

Vocabulary

VOCABULARY

The vocabulary presented here represents vocabulary as it is used in the contexts of the mini-dramas in this book. Some words will have different meanings in different contexts.

A

admission a statement saying that something is true
agronomist an expert in farming
Amtrak a major train system in the United States
anticipate to expect

B

balcony a place for people to stand or sit, built out on the upstairs wall of a building
ban to forbid
beach pass an admission ticket to a public beach, used by local beach towns as a tax
belch to burp, expel stomach gas through the mouth
bellboy a hotel employee who carries luggage; also *bellhop, bellman*
bicker to quarrel, or argue, about small matters
blush to become red in the face, from attention or shame
boardwalk an elevated wooden walkway along a beach or waterfront
bouquet a bunch of flowers
brew to mix with hot water and prepare for drinking
bride a woman about to be married or just married
broke without money (informal)
bureaucrat a government employee
busboy a restaurant employee who clears tables, brings water, etc.

C

carve to cut cooked meat into slices
casino a building used for playing games for money
casserole a combination of foods baked and served in a covered dish
catalog a book containing useful information
charge a spoken or written statement blaming a person for breaking the law
chili dog a hot dog sandwich with chili peppers and tomato sauce
cinnamon a sweet-smelling powder used for giving a special taste to food
classified a small advertisement put in a newspaper by a person who wants to buy or sell something, offer or get a job, etc.
clumsy awkward and ungraceful in movement
cold cuts assorted slices of cold meats
cold spell a short period of very cold temperatures
convenience store a small supermarket with long hours and short lines
cookout an informal meal cooked and eaten outdoors
cope to deal successfully with something
costume the clothes typical of a certain period, country, or profession

D

date a special social meeting between a man and woman, or boy and girl
dean an important officer at a college or university
delay to cause to be late
designated driver one person in a group of drinkers who promises not to drink alcoholic beverages in order to drive the rest home safely
diehard very enthusiastic and loyal
diner a small restaurant

115

dish a prepared food
down the road a piece not far away (informal)
downward going down
drastic strong, sudden, and severe
drumstick the lower part of the leg of a cooked bird
drunk overcome by alcohol, intoxicated
dude man (informal)
Dutch refers to people from Holland (the Netherlands)

E

eager full of interest
exhilarating lively, stimulating, enjoyable

F

fall apart to become unable to control one's feelings of sadness
fed a federal government employee
fine an amount of money paid as a punishment
fix to arrange unfairly or dishonestly
flatter to give pleasure to
floor horizontal division of a building, story
freshen up to feel more comfortable and attractive by washing

G

gamble to risk one's money on horse races, in games, etc.
get up for to become enthusiastic about
geyser a natural spring of hot water that from time to time rises suddenly into the air
ghost the spirit of a dead person who appears again
ginger ale a nonalcoholic soda
give up to stop working at or trying to do something
go back for seconds to help oneself to more food
go dutch each person pays his or her own expenses at an outing; also *dutch treat*
goodies good things to eat (informal)

groom a man about to be married or just married
guys people (informal)

H

hang out to spend time (informal)
happy hour a period in the late afternoon when many bars and restaurants lower the prices of their alcoholic beverages
hardship a difficult condition
have no idea to be confused about
hold up to survive, endure
homework school assignment to be done outside the classroom
hooked having a great liking for and very often using, doing, watching, etc.
hug to hold closely in one's arms, a sign of affection

I

I'll pass Skip me; I choose not to participate
idiom a phrase having a special meaning
illness a sickness
Indian refers to people from India (Some use the term to mean Native Americans.)
inflection a change in the voice according to the needs of expression
infraction a violation, or breaking, of a law

J

jargon the specialized language of a trade or profession
jittery nervous, uneasy
jumbled mixed up, in confusion
junk old, useless things
junk food snacks with little nutritional value

K

kickoff the start of a North American football game, when one team kicks the ball to the other

kid around to joke, especially with a friend

L

leash a rope, chain, or strap tied to a dog's collar to control it
leftovers food remaining uneaten after a meal
lift a ride
light something that will set a cigarette burning
light up to begin to smoke
literally according to the words and not the intention
living wage enough earnings to provide a reasonable level of comfort

M

make it to arrive
make little of to treat as unimportant
mall a large shopping center, often indoors
mask a covering for the face to hide or change it
merge to join
mingle to mix with people

N

nap a short sleep
neck of the woods an area or part of the country
nickname a name used informally instead of someone's own name

O

odd strange
on the house free
outfit clothes worn together
outgoing showing eagerness to mix socially with others
overdressed wearing clothes that are too formal

P

pay one's respects to offer sympathy to one in grief over another's death
period a division of a school day
pick on to criticize or blame
plant a factory
punctual prompt, on time
put (someone) on to play a joke on, deceive playfully

R

racquetball a game similar to tennis, played in a four-walled court
registration the act of enrolling in a school or a class
reimburse to pay back
rerun a showing of a program after its original showing
resort a vacation place
review a critical evaluation of a book, play, TV show, etc.
Revolutionary War the war between American colonies and Britain, which led to independence; also called the American Revolution
riddle a difficult and amusing question to which one must guess the answer
rise to come up
round up to gather together in one place
rummage sale a sale of used clothes and other things, often for a good cause such as helping the poor
run behind schedule to do something after the planned time

S

salad bar a table from which diners help themselves to fruits, vegetables, and other foods
sales slip a receipt given at a store
scan to read and record a price electronically
scuba an instrument used for breathing while swimming underwater
Seeing Eye dog a dog trained to lead a blind person

set   to go down
show the ropes   to teach someone the rules and customs of a place or activity
sitcom   short for *situation comedy*, a humorous TV show having standard characters who appear in different stories each week
softball   a game similar to baseball
stepfather   the husband of one's mother after the death or divorce of the father
story   a floor or level in a building
stubborn   determined, with a strong will
stuff   things (informal)
Sunbelt   the southern and southwestern states of the United States

T

tabloid   a newspaper with small pages, many pictures, and little serious news
ticket   a printed notice of an offense against driving laws
tint   a light coloring
to go   to be eaten outside the place where it was bought
top it off   to increase something, making it either better or worse
trade   related to the buying and selling of goods
traffic officer   a city employee in charge of enforcing parking laws
train   to give teaching and practice in a profession or skill
treat   something that gives pleasure
trick   something done to deceive or make someone look stupid
turkey   a bird, but in this context a friendly expression meaning "foolish person"
twins   two children born of the same mother at the same time

U

union   an association of workers
unnerve   to take away the courage of

V

vow   a promise

W

wake   a gathering to watch and grieve over a dead person on the night before the burial
well received   accepted and appreciated

Y

you bet   certainly, for sure

Daly City Public Library
Daly City, California

NTC ESL/EFL TEXTS AND MATERIAL
Junior High—Adult Education

Computer Software
Amigo
Basic Vocabulary Builder on Computer

Language and Culture Readers
Beginner's English Reader
Cultural Encounters in the U.S.A.
Passport to America series
  California Discovery
  Adventures in the Southwest
  The Coast-to-Coast Mystery
  The New York Connection
Discover America series
  (text/audiocassettes)
  California
  Chicago
  Florida
  Hawaii
  New England
  New York
  Texas
  Washington, D.C.
Looking at American Signs
Looking at American Food
Looking at American Recreation
Looking at American Holidays
Time: We the People (text/audiocassettes)

Text/Audiocassette Learning Packages
Speak Up! Sing Out! 1, 2
Listen and Say It Right in English!

Transparencies
Everyday Situations in English

Duplicating Masters and Blackline Masters
Easy Vocabulary Games
Vocabulary Games
Advanced Vocabulary Games
Play and Practice!
Basic Vocabulary Builder
Practical Vocabulary Builder
Beginning Activities for English
  Language Learners
Intermediate Activities for English
  Language Learners
Advanced Activities for English
  Language Learners

Language-Skills Texts
English with a Smile 1, 2
English Survival Series
  Building Vocabulary A, B, C
  Recognizing Details A, B, C
  Identifying Main Ideas A, B, C
  Writing Sentences and Paragraphs
    A, B, C
  Using the Context A, B, C
English Across the Curriculum 1, 2, 3
Essentials of Reading and Writing
  English 1, 2, 3
Everyday English 1, 2, 3, 4
Learning to Listen in English
  (workbook/audiocassettes)
Listening to Communicate in English
  (workbook/audiocassettes)

Communication Skillbooks 1, 2, 3
Living in the U.S.A. 1, 2, 3
Basic Everyday Spelling Workbook
  (audiocassettes)
Practical Everyday Spelling Workbook
  (audiocassettes)
Advanced Readings and Conversations
Practical English Writing Skills
Express Yourself in Written English
Campus English
Speak English!
Read English!
Write English!
Orientation in American English
Building English Sentences
Grammar for Use
Grammar Step-by-Step
Listening by Doing
Reading by Doing
Speaking by Doing
Vocabulary by Doing
Writing by Doing
Look, Think and Write

Survival-Skills Texts
Building Real Life English Skills
Everyday Consumer English
Book of Forms
Essential Life Skills series
Finding a Job in the United States
English for Adult Living 1, 2
Living in English
Prevocational English

TOEFL Preparation
NTC's Preparation Course for the
  TOEFL® (with 3 audiocassettes)
NTC's Practice Tests for the TOEFL®
  (with 3 audiocassettes)

Dictionaries and References
ABC's of Languages and Linguistics
Everyday American English Dictionary
Building Dictionary Skills in
  English (workbook)
Beginner's Dictionary of American
  English Usage
Beginner's English Dictionary
  Workbook
NTC's American Idioms Dictionary
NTC's Dictionary of American Slang
  and Colloquial Expressions
Essential American Idioms
Contemporary American Slang
Forbidden American English
101 American English Idioms
Idiom Workbook
Essentials of English Grammar
The Complete ESL/EFL Resource Book
Safari Grammar
Safari Punctuation
303 Dumb Spelling Mistakes
TESOL Professional Anthologies
  Grammar and Composition
  Listening, Speaking, and Reading
  Culture

For further information or a current catalog, write:
National Textbook Company
a division of *NTC Publishing Group*
4255 West Touhy Avenue
Lincolnwood, Illinois 60646-1975 U.S.A.